Practice Test #1

Practice Questions

English Test

<u>Passage 1</u>
Questions 1-30 pertain to the following passage:

The Washingtons (1) <u>had went</u> on many good vacations, but (2) <u>there</u> all-time favorite one was when they visited (3) <u>Mr. Washington's</u> cousin Lucy at her home by Lake Tahoe.

Mr. and Mrs. Washington and their kids Arlo and Ella (4) <u>piled onto the family car</u> surrounded by clothes and (5) <u>fishing equipments</u> and presents for (6) <u>Lucy and Lucys family</u>, (7) <u>rolled down their windows,</u> and drove away. Penny the dog came (8) <u>to</u> and sat on the seat (9) <u>next from Ella</u>. Ella was (10) <u>an avid painter,</u> so they brought her backpack with all her paints and brushes so she could do paintings of the lake.

They (11) <u>had been drive</u> for about two hours when they decided to stop for lunch. Mrs. Washington (12) <u>pulls the car of the highway</u> and stopped by a shady tree. (13) <u>As they getting out,</u> Mr. Washington grabbed a pen to use for (14) <u>filing in a crossword puzzle</u>. The pen leaked and he got a stripe of blue ink on his hand, which he absentmindedly wiped on his white t-shirt. (15) <u>Everybody get out of the car</u>, put down blankets to sit on, and got out the sandwiches and drinks. Penny (16) <u>drank all her food up</u> and lay down on the blanket for a nap in the sun. Arlo and Ella (17) <u>then decide</u> to climb the tree. Ella kept her backpack on when she climbed.

Under the tree, Mr. Washington was tired and lay down next to Penny who (18) <u>was dreaming and kick</u> in her sleep. He pulled his hat over his eyes and (19) <u>fell quick</u> asleep. Mrs. Washington enjoyed the quiet and (20) <u>read her book until she ate</u> her sandwich. Suddenly, a wasp flew close to her and (21) <u>startles</u> her, and she dropped her sandwich on Mr. Washington; mustard from her sandwich spilled on his shirt. She gasped, which (22) <u>woken up</u> Penny, who jumped into the tomato salad and fell against Mr. Washington with her paws covered in tomato juice. Ella was getting crackers (23) <u>in of</u> her backpack and looked down and laughed so hard at what (24) <u>she seen</u> that she dropped her backpack with the paints in it. The green paint did not have (25) <u>it's lid</u> screwed on tightly and fell on Mr. Washington next to the red, yellow, and blue marks, leaving a green mark.

Mr. Washington was (26) <u>wild awake</u> now and looking with (27) <u>surprised</u> at his shirt. Everyone else was laughing. Arlo then got sad that he (28) <u>hadn't help</u> color his dad's shirt, so he found a (29) <u>plumb</u> in the cooler and looked at his dad questioningly. Mr. Washington sighed and nodded with (30) <u>resignment</u>. Arlo bit the fruit and rubbed it on his dad's shirt.

When they got to Lake Tahoe, Lucy's four-year-old daughter came to the door and squealed when she saw them. She yelled to her mom, "Mom, Uncle Rainbow is here!" That's what she's called him ever since.

1. A. NO CHANGE
   B. has went
   C. gone
   D. had gone

2. F. NO CHANGE
   G. they're
   H. their
   J. theyre

3. A. NO CHANGE
   B. Mr. Washingtons'
   C. Mr. Washington
   D. Mr. Washington'

4. F. NO CHANGE
   G. piled into the family car
   H. piled atop the family car
   J. piling into the family car

5. A. NO CHANGE
   B. fishing equipment
   C. fishing equip
   D. equipments for fishing

6. F. NO CHANGE
   G. Lucy and Lucys' family
   H. Lucy and Lucy's family
   J. Lucy and their family

7. A. NO CHANGE
   B. rolled down his window
   C. rolled down their window
   D. rolled down windows

8. F. NO CHANGE
   G. two
   H. too
   J. though

9. A. NO CHANGE
   B. next by Ella
   C. next Ella
   D. next to Ella

- 4 -

10. F. NO CHANGE
    G. a avid painter
    H. her avid painter
    J. avidly a painter

11. A. NO CHANGE
    B. had drive
    C. had drived
    D. had been driving

12. F. NO CHANGE
    G. pulled the car off the highway
    H. pulled the car of the highway
    J. pulls the car off the highway

13. A. NO CHANGE
    B. As they were getting out
    C. As they get out
    D. As getting out

14. F. NO CHANGE
    G. filing a crossword puzzle
    H. filling in a crossword puzzle
    J. filing a crossword puzzle

15. A. NO CHANGE
    B. Everybody gets out of the car
    C. Everybody out of the car
    D. Everybody got out of the car

16. F. NO CHANGE
    G. drank her food
    H. ate all her food
    J. drank some of her food

17. A. NO CHANGE
    B. decide
    C. all decided
    D. then decided

18. F. NO CHANGE
    G. was dreaming and kicking
    H. dreamt and kick
    J. was dreaming of kicking

19. A. NO CHANGE
   B. fell quickly
   C. quick fell
   D. fall quickly

20. F. NO CHANGE
   G. read her book as she ate
   H. read her book, ate
   J. read her book and she ate

21. A. NO CHANGE
   B. startle
   C. startled
   D. was startling

22. F. NO CHANGE
   G. woke up
   H. awokened
   J. awakes

23. A. NO CHANGE
   B. in to
   C. from of
   D. out of

24. F. NO CHANGE
   G. she sees
   H. she saw
   J. she seeing

25. A. NO CHANGE
   B. its lid
   C. its' lid
   D. it lid

26. F. NO CHANGE
   G. wide awake
   H. wildly awake
   J. widely awake

27. A. NO CHANGE
   B. surprising
   C. surprise
   D. stupor

28. F. NO CHANGE
   G. had helped
   H. hadn't helped
   J. helped

29. A. NO CHANGE
    B. plum
    C. plump
    D. plumm

30. F. NO CHANGE
    G. resigned
    H. resigning
    J. resignation

Passage II
Questions 31-40 pertain to the following passage:

The media (31) covers a lot of (32) these kind of story. Do (33) to this reporting, people think it happens more often than (34) they really do. When (35) me and my group took a survey, a very small percentage (36) were personally familiar with it. Only a few individuals reported that this happened to themselves or anyone they (37) know (38) of. Analyzing the results, (39) most respondents had no experience with it. With such a small sample size, we can't say the sample is representative (40) to the population.

31. A. NO CHANGE
    B. cover
    C. covered
    D. covering

32. F. NO CHANGE
    G. this kinds
    H. these kinds
    J. this kind

33. A. NO CHANGE
    B. Done
    C. Due
    D. Does

34. F. NO CHANGE
    G. it really does
    H. they really did
    J. it really do

35. A. NO CHANGE
    B. my group and me
    C. I and my group
    D. my group and I

- 7 -

36. F. NO CHANGE
    G. are
    H. was
    J. is

37. A. NO CHANGE
    B. knew
    C. knows
    D. knowing

38. F. NO CHANGE
    G. anyone they know
    H. anyone of whom they knew
    J. anyone they knew about

39. A. NO CHANGE
    B. we found most respondents
    C. most of our respondents
    D. more of the respondents

40. F. NO CHANGE
    G. with
    H. of
    J. for

Mathematics Test

1. If $a = 3$ and $b = -2$, what is the value of $a^2 + 3ab - b^2$?
    A. 5
    B. -13
    C. -4
    D. -20
    E. 13

2. 34 is what percent of 80?
    F. 34%
    G. 40%
    H. 42.5%
    J. 44.5%
    K. 52%

3. Jack and Kevin play in a basketball game. If the ratio of points scored by Jack to points scored by Kevin is 4 to 3, which of the following could NOT be the total number of points scored by the two boys?
    A. 7
    B. 14
    C. 16
    D. 28
    E. 35

- 8 -

4. Factor the following expression: $x^2 + x - 12$
  F. $(x - 4)(x + 4)$
  G. $(x - 2)(x + 6)$
  H. $(x + 6)(x - 2)$
  J. $(x - 4)(x + 3)$
  K. $(x + 4)(x - 3)$

5. The average of six numbers is 4. If the average of two of those numbers is 2, what is the average of the other four numbers?
  A. 5
  B. 6
  C. 7
  D. 8
  E. 9

6. What is the next-highest prime number after 67?
  F. 68
  G. 69
  H. 71
  J. 73
  K. 76

7. Solve: 0.25 x 0.03 =
  A. 75
  B. 0.075
  C. 0.75
  D. 0.0075
  E. 7.5

8. Dean's Department Store reduces the price of a $30 shirt by 20%, but later raises it again by 20% of the sale price. What is the final price of the shirt?
  F. $24.40
  G. $32
  H. $30
  J. $28.80
  K. $26.60

9. How many 3-inch segments can a 4.5-yard line be divided into?
  A. 15
  B. 45
  C. 54
  D. 64
  E. 84

10. Sheila, Janice, and Karen, working together at the same rate, can complete a job in 3 1/3 days. Working at the same rate, how much of the job could Janice and Karen do in one day?
  F. 1/5
  G. 1/4
  H. 1/3
  J. 1/9
  K. 1/8

11. Dave can deliver four newspapers every minute. At this rate, how many newspapers can he deliver in 2 hours?
  A. 80
  B. 160
  C. 320
  D. 400
  E. 480

12. $4^6 \div 2^8 =$
  F. 2
  G. 8
  H. 16
  J. 32
  K. 64

13. If $a = 4$, $b = 3$, and $c = 1$, then $\dfrac{a(b - c)}{b(a + b + c)} =$
  A. 4/13
  B. 1/3
  C. 1/4
  D. 1/6
  E. 2/7

14. What is 20% of $\dfrac{12}{5}$, expressed as a percentage?
  F. 48%
  G. 65%
  H. 72%
  J. 76%
  K. 84%

15. Archie's gas tank is 1/3 full. If Archie adds 3 gallons of gas to the tank, it will be ½ full. What is the capacity in gallons of Archie's tank?
  A. 28
  B. 12
  C. 20
  D. 16
  E. 18

16. A boy has a spinner labeled with the numbers 1 – 10. He spins it 100 times and records his results in a table, shown below. Give the experimental probability that the boy will spin the number 6.

Number on Spinner	Frequency
1	12
2	15
3	11
4	6
5	12
6	14
7	8
8	10
9	12
10	3

    F. 6/100
    G. 100/100
    H. 10/100
    J. 14/100
    K. 4/100

17. Which of the following are complementary angles?
    A. 71° and 19°
    B. 18° and 18°
    C. 90° and 90°
    D. 90° and 45°
    E. 15° and 30°

18. A man decided to buy new furniture from Futuristic Furniture for $2600. Futuristic Furniture gave the man two choices: pay the entire amount in one payment with cash, or pay $1000 as a down payment and $120 per month for two full years in the financial plan. If the man chooses the financial plan, how much more would he pay?
    F. $1480 more
    G. $1280 more
    H. $1600 more
    J. $2480 more
    K. $3720 more

19. What is the value of r in the following equation?
$29 + r = 420$
    A. $r = 29/420$
    B. $r = 420/29$
    C. $r = 391$
    D. $r = 449$
    E. $r = 478$

20. Find the area of the rectangle.

5ft

7 ft

F. 5 ft²
G. 12 ft²
H. 24 ft²
J. 35 ft²
K. 70 ft²

21. If 35% of a paycheck was deducted for taxes and 4% for insurance, what is the total percent taken out of the paycheck?
    A. 20%
    B. 31%
    C. 39%
    D. 42%
    E. 48%

22. In the year 2000, 35% of the company sales were in electronics. The table below shows how electronic sales have changed for the company over the years. Find the percent of electronics sold in 2005.

Years	Change
2000 - 2001	-2
2001 - 2002	-1
2002 - 2003	+6
2003 - 2004	-1
2004 - 2005	+2

    F. 2%
    G. 11%
    H. 39%
    J. 42%
    K. 47%

23. Which of the following choices expresses 5/8 as a percent?
    A. 40%
    B. 58%
    C. 62.5%
    D. 65%
    E. 72%

24. In the following figure, angle b = 120°. What is the measurement of angle a?

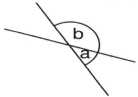

    F. 40°
    G. 60°
    H. 90°
    J. 100°
    K. 180°

25. The scientific notation for a red blood cell is approximately 7.4×10^{-4} centimeters in diameter. What is that amount in standard form?
    A. 0.00074
    B. 0.0074
    C. 7.40000
    D. 296
    E. -740000

26. A woman wants to stack two small bookcases beneath a window that is 26½ inches from the floor. The larger bookcase is 14½ inches tall. The other bookcase is 8¾ inches tall. How tall with the two bookcases be when they are stacked together?
    F. 12 inches tall
    G. 23¼ inches tall
    H. 35¼ inches tall
    J. 41 inches tall
    K. 49¾ inches tall

27. Solve for y in the following equation if $x = -3$
$y = x + 5$
    A. $y = -2$
    B. $y = 2$
    C. $y = 3$
    D. $y = 8$
    E. $y = 15$

28. Put the following integers in order from greatest to least:
-52, 16, -12, 14, 8, -5, 0
    F. -52, 16, -12, 14, 8, -5, 0
    G. 0, -5, 8, -12, 14, 16, -52
    H. 0, -5, -12, -52, 8, 14, 16
    J. 16, 14, 8, 0, -5, -12, -52
    K. -52, -12, -5, 0, 8, 14, 16

29. If number *x* is subtracted from 27, the result is -5. What is number *x*?
   A. 22
   B. 25
   C. 32
   D. 35
   E. 38

30. What is the simplest way to write the following expression?
5x – 2y + 4x + y
   F. $9x - y$
   G. $9x - 3y$
   H. $9x + 3y$
   J. $x ; y$
   K. $3x - y$

Reading Test

I. Prose Fiction

Questions 1 – 12 pertain to the following passage:

<u>Garth</u>

The next morning she realized that she had slept. This surprised her – so long had sleep been denied her! She opened her eyes and saw the sun at the window. And then, beside it in the window, the deformed visage of Garth. Quickly, she shut her eyes again, feigning sleep. But he was not fooled. Presently she heard his voice, soft and kind: "Don't be afraid. I'm your friend. I came to watch you sleep, is all. There now, I am behind the wall. You can open your eyes."

The voice seemed pained and plaintive. The Hungarian opened her eyes, saw the window empty. Steeling herself, she arose, went to it, and looked out. She saw the man below, cowering by the wall, looking grief-stricken and resigned. Making an effort to overcome her revulsion, she spoke to him as kindly as she could.

"Come," she said, but Garth, seeing her lips move, thought she was sending him away. He rose and began to lumber off, his eyes lowered and filled with despair.

"Come!" she cried again, but he continued to move off. Then, she swept from the cell, ran to him and took his arm. Feeling her touch, Garth trembled uncontrollably. Feeling that she drew him toward her, he lifted his supplicating eye and his whole face lit up with joy.

She drew him into the garden, where she sat upon a wall, and for a while they sat and contemplated one another. The more the Hungarian looked at Garth, the more deformities she discovered. The twisted spine, the lone eye, the huge torso over the tiny legs. She couldn't comprehend how a creature so awkwardly constructed could exist. And yet, from the air of sadness and gentleness that pervaded his figure, she began to reconcile herself to it.

"Did you call me back?" asked he.

- 14 -

"Yes," she replied, nodding. He recognized the gesture.

"Ah," he exclaimed. "Do you know that I am deaf?"

"Poor fellow," exclaimed the Hungarian, with an expression of pity.

"You'd think nothing more could be wrong with me," Garth put in, somewhat bitterly. But he was happier than he could remember having been.

1. Why was the girl surprised that she had slept?
   A. It was afternoon.
   B. She seldom slept.
   C. It had been a long time since she had had the chance to sleep.
   D. She hadn't intended to go to sleep.

2. Why did she shut her eyes again when she saw Garth in the window?
   F. She wanted to sleep some more.
   G. The sun was so bright that it hurt her eyes.
   H. She didn't want to look at Garth.
   J. She wanted Garth to think she was still sleeping.

3. What two characteristics are contrasted in Garth?
   A. Ugliness and gentleness
   B. Fear and merriment
   C. Distress and madness
   D. Happiness and sadness

4. During this passage, how do the girl's emotions toward Garth change?
   F. They go from fear to loathing.
   G. They go from anger to fear.
   H. They go from hatred to disdain.
   J. They go from revulsion to pity.

5. Why does the girl have to steel herself to approach the window and look out at Garth?
   A. She is groggy from sleep.
   B. She has not eaten for a long time.
   C. She is repelled by his appearance.
   D. She is blinded by the sun behind him.

6. How does Garth feel toward the girl when he first moves away from the window?
   F. He is curious about her.
   G. He is sad because she appears to reject him.
   H. He is angry at her for pretending to sleep.
   J. He pretends to be indifferent toward her.

7. Why does Garth withdraw from the girl when she first speaks to him?
   A. He expects her to hurt him.
   B. He misunderstands her because he cannot hear.
   C. People are always mean to him.
   D. He thinks she wants to sleep some more.

8. What is a synonym for the word *supplicating*?
   F. Castigating
   G. Menacing
   H. Repeating
   J. Begging

9. Why is it surprising that the girl takes Garth's arm?
   A. She is engaged to someone else.
   B. She has to reach through the window.
   C. He is deaf.
   D. She was very frightened of him initially.

10. Which of the following adjectives might you use to describe the girl's personality?
    F. Determined
    G. Robust
    H. Manic
    J. Sympathetic

11. Which of the following adjectives would you use to describe Garth's feelings toward himself?
    A. Contemplative
    B. Destitute
    C. Unhappy
    D. Deflated

12. Why is Garth so happy in the last sentence?
    F. Because he can understand the girl.
    G. He has learned to read lips.
    H. Because the girl figured out that he is deaf.
    J. Because the girl seems to accept him.

II. Social Sciences

Questions 13 – 24 pertain to the following passage:

New Zealand Inhabitants

The islands of New Zealand are among the most remote of all the Pacific islands. New Zealand is an archipelago, with two large islands and a number of smaller ones. Its climate is far cooler than the rest of Polynesia. Nevertheless, according to Maori legends, it was colonized in the early fifteenth century by a wave of Polynesian voyagers who traveled southward in their canoes and settled on North Island. At this time, New Zealand was already known to the Polynesians, who had probably first landed there some 400 years earlier.

The Polynesian southward migration was limited by the availability of food.

- 16 -

Traditional Polynesian tropical crops such as taro and yams will grow on North Island, but the climate of South Island is too cold for them. Coconuts will not grow on either island. The first settlers were forced to rely on hunting and gathering, and, of course, fishing. Especially on South Island, most settlements remained close to the sea. At the time of the Polynesian influx, enormous flocks of moa birds had their rookeries on the island shores. These flightless birds were easy prey for the settlers, and within a few centuries had been hunted to extinction. Fish, shellfish and the roots of the fern were other important sources of food, but even these began to diminish in quantity as the human population increased. The Maori had few other sources of meat: dogs, smaller birds, and rats. Archaeological evidence shows that human flesh was also eaten, and that tribal warfare increased markedly after the moa disappeared.

By far the most important farmed crop in prehistoric New Zealand was the sweet potato. This tuber is hearty enough to grow throughout the islands, and could be stored to provide food during the winter months, when other food-gathering activities were difficult. The availability of the sweet potato made possible a significant increase in the human population. Maori tribes often lived in encampments called *pa*, which were fortified with earthen embankments and usually located near the best sweet potato farmlands.

13. A definition for the word *archipelago* is
    A. A country
    B. A place in the southern hemisphere
    C. A group of islands
    D. A roosting place for birds

14. This article is primarily about what?
    F. The geology of New Zealand
    G. New Zealand's early history
    H. New Zealand's prehistory
    J. Food sources used by New Zealand's first colonists.

15. According to the passage, when was New Zealand first settled?
    A. In the fifteenth century
    B. Around the eleventh century
    C. Thousands of years ago
    D. By flightless birds

16. Why did early settlements remain close to the sea?
    F. The people liked to swim.
    G. The people didn't want to get far from the boats they had come in.
    H. Taro and yams grow only close to the beaches.
    J. They were dependent upon sea creatures for their food.

17. Why do you suppose tribal warfare increased after the moa disappeared?
   A. Increased competition for food led the people to fight.
   B. Some groups blamed others for the moa's extinction.
   C. They had more time on their hands since they couldn't hunt the moa, so they fought.
   D. One group was trying to consolidate political control over the entire country.

18. How did the colder weather of New Zealand make it difficult for the Polynesians to live there?
   F. The Polynesians weren't used to making warm clothes.
   G. Cold water fish are harder to catch.
   H. Some of them froze.
   J. Some of their traditional crops would not grow there.

19. What was a significant difference between the sweet potato and other crops known to the Polynesians?
   A. The sweet potato provided more protein.
   B. The sweet potato would grow on North Island.
   C. The sweet potato could be stored during the winter.
   D. The sweet potato could be cultured near their encampments.

20. Why was it important that sweet potatoes could be stored?
   F. They could be eaten in winter, when other foods were scarce.
   G. They could be traded for fish and other goods.
   H. They could be taken along by groups of warriors going to war.
   J. They tasted better after a few weeks of storage.

21. Why do you suppose the *pa* were usually located near sweet potato farmlands?
   A. So they could defend the best farmlands from their fortified camps.
   B. So they could have ready access to their most important source of food.
   C. So they could transport the potatoes easily into camp for storage.
   D. All of the above are probably true.

22. Why might the shellfish populations have diminished as the human population increased?
   F. Too many people poisoned the waters.
   G. The shellfish didn't like people and migrated elsewhere.
   H. The people were hunting the natural predators of the shellfish to extinction.
   J. The humans were eating the shellfish faster than they could replenish themselves through reproduction.

23. What was it about the moa that made them easy for the Maori to catch?
   A. They were fat.
   B. They roosted by the shore.
   C. They were not very smart.
   D. They were unable to fly.

24. What might have been one of the reasons that the Maori practiced cannibalism?
    F. They were starving so they turned to human flesh.
    G. The Polynesians had a tradition of cannibalism, which they brought with them to New Zealand.
    H. Human flesh tasted a lot like moa.
    J. They were fighting over the sweet potato farmlands.

III. Humanities

Questions 25 – 30 pertain to the following passage:

The Coins of Ancient Greece

We don't usually think of coins as works of art, and most of them really do not invite us to do so. The study of coins, their development and history, is termed *numismatics*. Numismatics is a topic of great interest to archeologists and anthropologists, but not usually from the perspective of visual delectation. The coin is intended, after all, to be a utilitarian object, not an artistic one. Many early Greek coins are aesthetically pleasing as well as utilitarian, however, and not simply because they are the earliest examples of the coin design. Rather, Greek civic individualism provides the reason. Every Greek political entity expressed its identity through its coinage.

The idea of stamping metal pellets of a standard weight with an identifying design had its origin on the Ionian Peninsula around 600 B.C. Each of the Greek city-states produced its own coinage adorned with its particular symbols. The designs were changed frequently to commemorate battles, treaties, and other significant occasions. In addition to their primary use as a pragmatic means of facilitating commerce, Greek coins were clearly an expression of civic pride. The popularity of early coinage led to a constant demand for new designs, such that there arose a class of highly skilled artisans who took great pride in their work, so much so that they sometimes even signed it. As a result, Greek coins provide us not only with an invaluable source of historical knowledge, but also with a genuine expression of the evolving Greek sense of form, as well. These minuscule works reflect the development of Greek sculpture from the sixth to the second century B.C. as dependably as do larger works made of marble or other metals. And since they are stamped with the place and date of their production, they provide an historic record of artistic development that is remarkably dependable and complete.

25. What is the purpose of this passage?
    A. To attract new adherents to numismatics as a pastime.
    B. To show how ancient Greeks used coins in commerce.
    C. To teach the reader that money was invented in Greece.
    D. To describe ancient Greek coinage as an art form

26. What is meant by the phrase "most of them do not invite us to do so", as used in the first sentence?
    F. Money is not usually included when sending an invitation.
    G. Most coins are not particularly attractive.
    H. Invitations are not generally engraved onto coins.
    J. Coins do not speak.

- 19 -

27. What is a synonym for "delectation", as used in the third sentence?
    A. Savoring
    B. Choosing
    C. Deciding
    D. Refusing

28. What is meant by the term numismatics?
    F. The study of numbers
    G. Egyptian history
    H. Greek history
    J. The study of coins

29. According to the text, how do ancient Greek coins differ from most other coinage?
    A. Simply because they were the first coins.
    B. Each political entity made its own coins.
    C. They were made of precious metals.
    D. They were designed with extraordinary care.

30. How often were new coins designed in ancient Greece?
    F. Monthly
    G. Not very often.
    H. Whenever there was a significant occasion to commemorate.
    J. When the old ones wore out.

Science Test

PART A

Questions 1-8 are based upon the following figure, table, and text:

Most particles studied by physicists are unstable. Given enough time, an unstable particle will break apart into two or more smaller particles or fragments. This event is called a decay. By carefully observing and logically classifying these decays according to some well-understood laws of nature, particle physicists have built a catalog of subatomic particles down to their most fundamental constituent parts.

Some particles, like the proton and electron, appear to be stable for very long times. They don't change into other particles, which is to say they don't decay. Most other particles have dominant decay modes. They decay into one combination of particles more often than into other combinations. Many particles also have rare decay modes. Someone who has the patience to watch a million or so decays, might see one of these rare combinations.

Two of the laws of nature that have been used to understand decays are *conservation of charge* and *conservation of energy*. Conservation of charge says that the net charge of all particles produced in a decay should equal the total charge of the original particle. Conservation of energy implies that the total mass of the resulting particles should not be greater than the mass of the original particle. Mass does not seem to be conserved in many decays until one accounts for the mass that is converted into the kinetic energy of the resulting particles as they move away

- 20 -

from the original center of mass at some nonzero speed. Mass and energy can be measured with the same units: particle physicists use MeV (1.000 mega-electron volt = 1.602 x 10^{-13} joule = 1.783 x 10^{-30} kilogram).

At the most fundamental level, matter is thought to be made up of quarks and leptons. Quarks form the large baryons and mesons. There are six quarks named up (u), down (d), strange (s), charm (c), bottom (b), and top (t). (The last two are sometimes fancifully referred to as "beauty" and "truth.") Each comes in three "colors" and each has an antiparticle making 36 in all. The six quarks have been confirmed through indirect observations, but not isolated as individual particles.

Refer to the accompanying table of subatomic particles to answer the questions.

Table:

HADRONS - made of quarks

* BARYONS - made of three quarks or three anti-quarks
NUCLEONS - contain no strange quarks

PARTICLE	CHARGE	MASS(MeV)
proton	1	938.27231
anti-proton	-1	938.27231
neutron	0	939.56563
anti-neutron	0	939.56563

HYPERONS - contain one or more strange quarks

PARTICLE	CHARGE	MASS(MeV)
lambda	0	1115.684
anti-lambda	0	1115.684
positive sigma	1	1189.37
anti-positive sigma	-1	1189.37
neutral sigma	0	1192.55
anti-neutral sigma	0	1192.55
negative sigma	-1	1197.436
anti-negative sigma	1	1197.436
neutral xi	0	1314.9
anti-neutral xi	0	1314.9
negative xi	-1	1321.32
anti-negative xi	1	1321.32
negative omega	-1	1672.45
positive omega	1	1672.45

* MESONS - made of one quark and one anti-quark

PARTICLE	CHARGE	MASS(MeV)
positive pion	1	139.56995
negative pion	-1	139.56995
neutral pion	0	134.9764
positive kaon	1	493.677
negative kaon	-1	493.677
neutral kaon	0	497.672
anti-neutral kaon	0	497.672

eta	0	547.45

LEPTONS - elementary particles not made of quarks

PARTICLE	CHARGE	MASS(MeV)
positron	1	0.51099907
electron	-1	0.51099907
electron neutrino	0	0
electron anti-neutrino	0	0
positive muon	1	105.658389
negative muon	-1	105.658389
muon neutrino	0	0
muon anti-neutrino	0	0
positive tau	1	1777
negative tau	-1	1777
tau neutrino	0	0
tau anti-neutrino	0	0

1. Which of the following particles has the greatest mass?
   A. Muon
   B. Electron
   C. Proton
   D. Lambda

2. Which of the following particles are made of quarks?
   F. Neutrino
   G. Muon
   H. Proton
   J. Tau

3. When a particle decays, the total charge on the resulting particles must always
   A. be neutral
   B. be equal to 0
   C. satisfy the law of conservation of mass
   D. be equal to the charge of the original particle

4. The most massive uncharged particles are found among the
   F. Leptons
   G. Mesons
   H. Baryons
   J. Hyperons

5. A lambda particle decays and one of the products is a proton. A second particle is also formed. Which of the following is the second particle?
   A. Negative pion
   B. Positron
   C. Electron neutrino
   D. Neutron

6. A positive muon decays and one of the products is a positron. If a second particle is also formed, which of the following might it be?

    F. Proton

    G. Tau

    H. Neutrino

    J. Kaon

7. A negative omega particle decays into a lambda particle and a negative kaon. How much energy is released?

    A. 63.09 MeV

    B. 1115.68 MeV

    C. 493.68 MeV

    D. 1672.45 MeV

8. Tom weighs 60 kilograms. What is his mass in MeV?

    F. 6×10^{11}

    G. 33.65×10^{30}

    H. 60

    J. 132

PART B

Questions 9-14 are based upon the following figure, table, and text:

Protein Synthesis

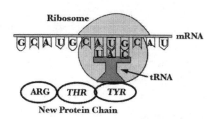

- 23 -

The Genetic Code

First	Codon	AA	Codon	AA	Codon	AA	Codon	AA
T	TTT	Phenylalanine	TCT	Serine	TAT	Tyrosine	TGT	Cysteine
	TTC	Phenylalanine	TCC	Serine	TAC	Tyrosine	TGC	Cysteine
	TTA	Leucine	TCA	Serine	TAA	STOP	TGA	STOP
	TTG	Leucine	TCG	Serine	TAG	STOP	TGG	Tryptophane
C	CTT	Leucine	CCT	Proline	CAT	Histidine	CGT	Arginine
	CTC	Leucine	CCC	Proline	CAC	Histidine	CGC	Arginine
	CTA	Leucine	CCA	Proline	CAA	Glycine	CGA	Arginine
	CTG	Leucine	CCG	Proline	CAG	Glycine	CGG	Arginine
A	ATT	Isoleucine	ACT	Threonine	AAT	Asparagine	AGT	Serine
	ATC	Isoleucine	ACC	Threonine	AAC	Asparagine	AGC	Serine
	ATA	Isoleucine	ACA	Threonine	AAA	Lysine	AGA	Arginine
	ATG	Methionine (START)	ACG	Threonine	AAG	Lysine	AGG	Arginine
G	GTT	Valine	GCT	Alanine	GAT	Aspartate	GGT	Glycine
	GTC	Valine	GCC	Alanine	GAC	Aspartate	GGC	Glycine
	GTA	Valine	GCA	Alanine	GAA	Glutamate	GGA	Glycine
	GTG	Valine	GCG	Alanine	GAG	Glutamate	GGG	Glycine

The genetic information for making different kinds of proteins is stored in segments of DNA molecules called genes. DNA is a chain of phosphoribose molecules containing the bases guanine (G), cytosine (C), alanine (A), and thymine (T). Each amino acid component of the protein chain is represented in the DNA by a trio of bases called a codon. This provides a code, which the cell can use to translate DNA into protein. The code, which is shown in the table, contains special codons for starting a protein chain (these chains always begin with the amino acid methionine), or for stopping it. To make a protein, an RNA intermediary called a messenger RNA (mRNA) is first made from the DNA by a protein called a polymerase. In the mRNA, the thymine bases are replaced by uracil (U). The mRNA then moves from the nucleus to the cytoplasm, where it locks onto a piece of protein-RNA machinery called a ribosome. The ribosome moves along the RNA molecule, reading the code. It interacts with molecules of transfer RNA, each of which is bound to a specific amino acid, and strings the amino acids together to form a protein.

9. Gene variants are called:
   A. Codons
   B. Alleles
   C. Methionine
   D. Amino acids

10. Which of the following protein sequences is encoded by the DNA base sequence GTTACAAAAAGA?
    F. Valine-threonine-lysine-arginine
    G. Valine-leucine-glycine-histidine
    H. Valine-aspartate-proline-serine
    J. Valine-serine-tyrosine-STOP

11. A polymerase begins reading the following DNA sequences with the first base shown. Which sequence specifies the end of a protein chain?
    A. GTACCCCTA
    B. GTACCCACA
    C. GTTAAAAGA
    D. GTTTAAGAC

12. The portion of a DNA molecule that encodes a single amino acid is a(n):
    F. Codon
    G. Allele
    H. Methionine
    J. Phosphoribose

13. Proteins are made by:
    A. Polymerases
    B. Transfer RNAs
    C. Ribosomes
    D. DNA molecules

14. Which of the following is NOT part of a gene?
    F. Guanine
    G. Codon
    H. Cytosine
    J. Ribosome

PART C

Questions 15-17 are based upon the following figure and text:
Electrochemical Battery

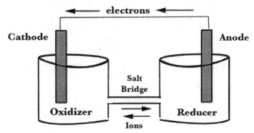

An electrochemical battery is a device powered by oxidation and reduction reactions that are physically separated so that the electrons must travel through a wire from the reducing agent to the oxidizing agent. The reducing agent loses electrons, and is oxidized in a reaction that takes place at an electrode called the

- 25 -

anode. The electrons flow through a wire to the other electrode, the cathode, where an oxidizing agent gains electrons and is thus reduced. To maintain a net zero charge in each compartment, there is a limited flow of ions through a salt bridge. In a car battery, for example, the reducing agent is oxidized by the following reaction, which involves a lead (Pb) anode and sulfuric acid (H_2SO_4). Lead sulfate ($PbSO_4$), protons (H^+), and electrons (e^-) are produced:

$Pb + H_2SO_4 \Rightarrow PbSO_4 + 2 H^+ + 2 e^-$

At the cathode, which is made of lead oxide (PbO_2), the following reaction occurs. During this reaction, the electrons produced at the anode are used:

$PbO_2 + H_2SO_4 + 2 e^- + 2 H^+ \Rightarrow PbSO_4 + 2 H_2O$

15. Electrons are produced by a chemical reaction that takes place at the:
   A. Anode
   B. Cathode
   C. Lead oxide electrode
   D. Oxidizer

16. In an oxidation reaction:
   F. An oxidizing agent gains electrons.
   G. An oxidizing agent loses electrons.
   H. A reducing agent gains electrons.
   J. A reducing agent loses electrons.

17. In a car battery, a product of the oxidation reaction that occurs at the cathode is:
   A. Lead oxide
   B. Lead
   C. Electrons
   D. Water

PART D

Questions 18-21 are based upon the following figure and text:

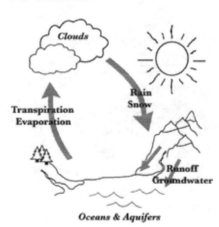

THE WATER CYCLE

Energy from the sun heats the water in the oceans and causes it to evaporate,

- 26 -

forming water vapor that rises through the atmosphere. Cooler temperatures at high altitudes cause this vapor to condense and form clouds. Water droplets in the clouds condense and grow, eventually falling to the ground as precipitation. This continuous movement of water above and below ground is called the hydrologic cycle, or water cycle, and it is essential for life on our planet. All the Earth's stores of water, including that found in clouds, oceans, underground, etc., are known as the *hydrosphere*.

Water can be stored in several locations as part of the water cycle. The largest reservoirs are the oceans, which hold about 95% of the world's water, more than 300,000,000 cubic miles. Water is also stored in polar ice caps, mountain snowcaps, lakes and streams, plants, and below ground in aquifers. Each of these reservoirs has a characteristic *residence time*, which is the average amount of time a water molecule will spend there before moving on. Some typical residence times are shown in the table.

Average reservoir residence times of water

Reservoir	Residence Time
Atmosphere	days 9
Oceans	3000 years
Glaciers and ice caps	years 100
Soil moisture	months 2
Underground aquifers	10,000 years

The water cycle can change over time. During cold climatic periods, more water is stored as ice and snow, and the rate of evaporation is lower. This affects the level of the Earth's oceans. During the last ice age, for instance, oceans were 400 feet lower than today. Human activities that affect the water cycle include agriculture, dam construction, deforestation, and industrial activities.

18. Another name for the water cycle is:
    F. The hydrosphere
    G. The atmosphere
    H. The reservoir
    J. The hydrologic cycle

19. Water is stored underground, as well as in oceans and ice caps. Such underground storage reservoirs are called:
    A. Storage tanks
    B. Aquifers
    C. Evaporators
    D. Runoff

20. Other than atmospheric water, water molecules spend the least time in:
    F. Aquifers
    G. Oceans
    H. Glaciers
    J. Soil

21. Which of the following statements is NOT true?
    A. Cutting down trees affects the water cycle.
    B. Ocean levels rise during an ice age.
    C. Oceans hold most of the world's water.
    D. Clouds are formed because of cold temperatures.

PART E

Questions 22-26 are based upon the following figure and text:
Heat and the States of Matter

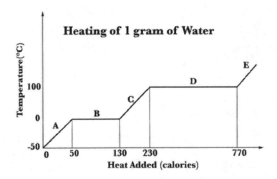

When the molecules of a substance absorb energy in the form of heat, they begin to move more rapidly. This increase in kinetic energy may be a more rapid vibration of molecules held in place in a solid, or it may be motion through molecular space in a liquid or a gas. Either way, it will be observed as either a change in temperature or a change in state. Heat has traditionally been measured in terms of calories. One calorie is equal to 4.186 Joules.

The specific heat capacity of a substance is the energy required to raise the temperature of 1 kg of the substance by 1°C. For water, this is 1000 calories. If heat continues to be applied to ice that is already at its melting point of 0°C, it remains at that temperature and melts into liquid water. The amount of energy required to produce this change in state is called the heat of fusion, and for water it is equal to 80 calories per gram. Similarly, the amount of energy required to change a gram of liquid water at 100°C into steam is called the heat of vaporization, and equals 540 calories.

The graph shows an experiment in calorimetry: 1 gram of water at -50°C is heated slowly from a solid state until it has all turned to gas. The temperature is monitored and reported as a function of the heat added to the system.

22. Heat is a form of:
    F. Potential energy
    G. Chemical energy
    H. Kinetic energy
    J. Temperature

23. Which of the following statements is true?
    A. Adding heat to a system always increases its temperature.
    B. The average speed of a gas molecule is slower than the average speed of a liquid molecule of the same substance.
    C. Adding heat to a system always increases the average speed of the molecules of which it is comprised.
    D. Heat must be added to liquid water to make ice.

24. In the diagram, in which region(s) of the diagram is liquid water present?
    F. B only
    G. B and C
    H. C only
    J. B, C, and D

25. How much heat must be added to 1 gram of water at 1°C to raise its temperature to 101°C?
    A. 100 calories
    B. 540 calories
    C. 770 calories
    D. 640 calories

26. In the diagram, as heat is added to the system, the water in region B can be said to be:
    F. Condensing
    G. Melting
    H. Freezing
    J. Evaporating

PART F

Questions 27-30 are based upon the following figure and text:

The basic functional cell is a neuron. Most neurons have small cell bodies and long extensions called axons and dendrites. Axons send information to target cells, while dendrites are the sites for receiving information. The nervous system also contains glial cells that support and nourish neurons. Some glial cells produce an insulating material called myelin. There may be ten times as many glial cells as neurons.

The message that passes down the dendrites through the cell body, and then away from the cell along axons, is electrical. At the end of the axon, the message changes. Between the terminal of one cell's axon and the dendrite of the next cell there is a tiny gap, called a synapse. The membrane there is able to release specialized chemicals called neurotransmitters. These chemicals jump the gap to the next cell, exciting the membrane of the nearest dendrite(s). That stimulus creates another electrical response, and the chain message continues.

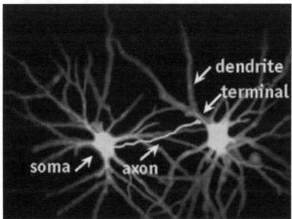

--From National Institute of Mental Health, 2010 (www.nimh.gov)

27. The part of a cell in the nervous system that sends messages is a(n)
    A. dendrite
    B. neuron
    C. axon
    D. terminal

28. The part of a cell in the nervous system that receives messages is a(n)
    F. neuron
    G. dendrite
    H. synapse
    J. axon

29. The space where communication between nerve cells occurs is a(n)
    A. synapse
    B. neuron
    C. axon
    D. dendrite

30. The protective myelin sheath around nerve cells is produced by
    F. cell membranes
    G. glial cells
    H. neurotransmitters
    J. cell bodies

Answers and Explanations

English Test

Passage I

1. D: The correct verb tense in this sentence is the past perfect tense with "gone" rather than "went."

2. H: "Their" is the correct word when indicating a possessive form of they.

3. A: This sentence correctly uses the possessive case.

4. G: As a car is something people enter rather than sit on top of, the correct answer is the one that indicates that the family, in the past, got into the car.

5. B: Equipment should be singular.

6. H: The option is the correct form of the possessive case for a singular noun (Lucy).

7. A: This sentence as written correctly uses the possessive form of they.

8. H: "Too" is the correct spelling of the word meaning also.

9. D: "Next to Ella" is the grammatically correct way to indicate this physical proximity.

10. F: The sentence is correct as written.

11. D: The tense needed here is past perfect progressive (indicating ongoing action completed at a definite time). Answer D is the only option with the correct tense.

12. G: The action happened in the past so the correct verb tense is "pulled." One gets off a highway rather than of a highway.

13. B: Need the indication of past tense that the "were" provides.

14. H: One fills in a crossword puzzle, rather than files in a crossword puzzle.

15. D: The action happened in the past, so the past tense version of the verb is correct.

16. H: One eats their food rather than drinks it.

17. D: The action happened in the past, so the past tense version of the verb is correct.

18. G: The verb forms should be parallel.

19. B: The phrase occurred in the past so "fell" is the correct verb tense. Quick needs to be in the form of an adverb to modify the verb fell, so "quickly" is correct.

- 31 -

20. G: The sentence is awkward and doesn't make sense as written. It makes sense if the sentence is written so that the two actions happen simultaneously.

21. C: The action happened in the past, so the past tense version of the verb is correct.

22. G: The only correct verb form of the options given is woke up.

23. D: The correct expression is "out of" when one is removing something from a container.

24. H: The action happened in the past, so the past tense version of the verb is correct.

25. B: The possessive form of it is its.

26. G: The correct expression is wide awake.

27. C: The word sought must be a noun and surprise fits the context better than stupor.

28. H: The verb tense needed is past perfect, indicating a completed action.

29. B: The correct spelling of the fruit is "plum."

30. J: The sentence requires a noun that one experiences when feeling resigned. The correct word is resignation.

Passage II

31. B: The word "media" is plural. It is a common error to use it as singular. The correct singular is "medium." (The same is true of "datum" and "data." These endings come from Latin roots.) Thus it should be "media cover," not "covers." Past tense changes the meaning. The participle "covering" would not be grammatical in this sentence without adding the linking verb "are."

32. J: The noun "kind" is singular, so the definite article modifying it should be "this," not "these." The plurals in "these kinds" would only be correct if the noun in the prepositional phrase were also plural, e.g., "these kinds of stories."

33. C: The correct spelling is "due." "Due to" means owing to, because of, etc. It is a frequent error to confuse the spelling of "due," an adjective also having common usage as a prepositional phrase in "due to," with the spelling of "do," a verb (to do), and vice versa.

34. G: The phrase "it happens more often than it really does" has the correct subject-verb agreement in number (singular = "it") and tense (present = "happens," "does"). "They" is plural; "did" is past tense; and "do" is plural, so these do not agree.

35. D: When connecting "I" or "me" to another person's name or description, the rule is always to put the other's name or description first. "I and my group" violates this rule and is incorrect. "My group and me" is also incorrect because the part of the sentence subject without "my group" is "I." not "me." "Me and my group" is incorrect for both reasons above.

36. H: "A...percentage" is a singular noun preceded by a singular article. Hence the verb should be singular ("was," not "were"). "Are" is not only plural but is also present tense, disagreeing with the

- 32 -

past tense verb "took."

37. B: The sentence construction is past tense. ("When [we] took a survey,...") "Know" is present tense; "knows" is present tense and singular, disagreeing with the phrase subject "they." "Knowing" is a participial form requiring a copula ("are" or "were").

38. H: This construction can seem cumbersome and is not often used, but it is the only correct choice here. Choice J and the original are incorrect by ending a sentence with a preposition ("of," "about"). Choice G changes the meaning: knowing anyone differs from knowing *of* anyone. Note: Because "of whom they knew" sounds awkward, it would be better to word this differently, e.g., "...this happened to themselves or others."

39. B: The original has a dangling participle. "Analyzing the results" refers to us (my group and me), not to "respondents," so the subject ("we") and verb ("found") are needed.

40. H: The phrase "representative of the population" uses a more appropriate choice of preposition than "representative to the population," "representative with the population," or "representative for the population."

Mathematics Test

1. B: Simply substitute the given values for *a* and *b* and perform the required operations.

2. H: This problem is solved by finding *x* in this equation: $34/80 = x/100$.

3. C: Every possible combination of scores is a multiple of 7, since the two terms of the ratio have a sum of seven.

4. K: To solve this problem, work backwards. That is, perform FOIL on each answer choice until you derive the original expression.

5. A: A set of six numbers with an average of 4 must have a collective sum of 24. The two numbers that average 2 will add up to 4, so the remaining numbers must add up to 20. The average of these four numbers can be calculated: $20/4 = 5$.

6. H: Prime numbers are those that are only evenly divisible by one and themselves.

7. D: Simple Multiplication.

8. J: Multiply 30 by 0.2 and subtract this from the original price of the shirt to find the sale price: $24. Then multiply 24 by 0.2 and add the product to the sale price to find the final price.

9. C: There are 12 inches in a foot and 3 feet in a yard. Four and a half yards is equal to 162 inches. To determine the number of 3-inche segments, divide 162 by 3.

10. F: If it takes 3 people 3 1/3 days to do the job, then it would take one person 10 days: $3 \times 3\frac{1}{3} = 10$. Thus, it would take 2 people 5 days, and one day of work for two people would

- 33 -

complete 1/5 of the job.

11. E: There are 60 minutes in an hour, so Dave can deliver 240 newspapers every hour. In 2 hours, then, he can deliver 480 papers.

12. H: Since 4 is the same as 2^2, $4^6 = 2^{12}$. When dividing exponents with the same base, simply subtract the exponent in the denominator from the exponent in the numerator.

13. B: Substitute the given values and solve. Resolve the parenthetical operations first.

14. F: Convert 20% to the fraction 1/5, then multiply by 12/5. The resulting fraction, 12/25, must have both numerator and denominator multiplied by 4 to become a percentage.

15. E: This problem can be solved with the following equation, in which x = the total capacity of the tank: $\frac{1}{2}x = \frac{1}{3}x + 3$.

16. J: Experimental probability is a ratio of how many times the spinner will land on the specific number to the total number of times the spinner is spun. In this case, the boy landed on the number 6 a total of 14 times. He tried the spinner 100 times. The resulting ratio is 14/100.

17. A: Complementary angles are two angles that equal 90° when added together.

18. G: Multiply $120 by 24 months (a full two years) to get $2880. Add the thousand dollars for the down payment to get $3880. Find the difference between the entire amount all at once ($2600) and the amount pain in the plan ($3800). To find the difference, you subtract. The difference shows that $1280 more is paid with the installment plan.

19. C: $29 + r = 420$
$29 + r - 29 = 420 - 29$
$r = 391$

20. J: Area = length x width
$A = 7 \times 5$
$A = 35$

21. C: To solve, find the sum. 35% + 4% = 39%

22. H: Electronics sales = x
$x = 35 + (-2) + (-1) + (+6) + (-1) + (+2)$
$x = (35 + 6 + 2) + (-2 + (-1) + (-1))$
$x = (43) + (-4)$
$x = 39$

23. C: Solve as follows:
$5/8 = x/100$
$5 \cdot 100 \div 8 = x$
$x = 62.5$

24. G: These are supplementary angles. That means that the two angles will add up to a total of 180°, which is the angle of a straight line. To solve, subtract as follows:

b = 180° - 120°

b = 60°

25. A: To solve, you will need to move the decimal 4 places. Since the scientific notation had a negative power of 10, move the decimal left. If the power of 10 had been positive, you would have needed to move it to the right. In this problem, solve as follows:

7.4×10^{-4}

$7.4 \times 1/10,000$

7.4×0.0001

0.00074

26. G: Add to solve. The height of the window from the floor is not needed in this equation. It is extra information. You only need to add the heights of the two bookcases. Change the fractions so that they have a common denominator. After you add, simply the fraction.

$14\frac{1}{2} + 8\frac{3}{4}$

$= 14 \ 2/4 + 8\frac{3}{4}$

$= 22 \ 5/4$

$= 23\frac{1}{4}$

27. B: $y = x + 5$, and you were told that $x = -3$. Fill in the missing information for x, then solve.

$y = (-3) + 5$

$y = 2$

28. J: Think of the numbers as they would be on a number line to place them in the correct order.

29. C: In this problem, if you do not know how to solve, try filling in the answer choices to see which one checks out. Many math problems may be solved by a guess and check method when you have a selection of answer choices.

$27 - x = -5$

$x = 32$

30. F: Add the numbers with x together, as follows: 5x + 4x = 9x

Add the y numbers, as follows: -2y + y = -y

Put the x and y numbers back into the same equation: 9x – y.

Reading Test

Prose Fiction

1. C: In the first sentence the phrase "so long had sleep been denied her" tells us she had been prevented from sleeping for some time.

2. J: The text tells us she was feigning, which means to pretend, to be asleep.

3. A: Despite his ugliness and deformity, Garth is a gentle soul who wants to be accepted as a friend by the girl.

4. J: At first repelled by the sight of Garth in the window, the girl eventually expresses pity when she learns that he is deaf, too.

5. C: Garth's deformities are repugnant to her at first, and she must overcome this emotion.

6. G: He calls back to her that he is hidden from sight, and his voice is described as plaintive and pained.

7. B: The text tells us that he sees her lips move and assumes she is sending him away, because he cannot hear that she is calling to him.

8. J: 9. D: At first she was amazed at the extent of Garth's deformities, but she has quickly become more sympathetic and has come to pity him

10. J: The girl quickly understands Garth's sadness about his own condition and sympathizes with him.

11. C: Garth is sad that he is so deformed that other people are frequently repelled and try to avoid contact with him.

12. J: The girl has shown that she sympathizes with him by taking his arm, and Garth feels that he is being accepted despite his deformities.

Social Science

13. C: An archipelago is a large group or chain of islands.

14. J: The article deals primarily with the ways the colonists fed themselves: their crops and the foods they hunted. While it also describes New Zealand's prehistory, the main focus is on food sources.

15. B: The article states that the islands were colonized by Polynesians in the fifteenth century but that the first settlers had arrived some 400 years earlier than that.

16. J: The passage states that the first settlers were forced to rely on fishing for their food.

17. A: When an increased population had driven a major food source to extinction, they began to fight for control over the remaining food supply.

18. J: The article tells us that coconuts did not grow in New Zealand, and that some of the other crops would grow only on North Island.

19. C: The sweet potato could be stored, providing a source of food during the winter when other food gathering activities were difficult.

20. F: The sweet potato provided a winter food source through storage, allowing the population to increase.

21. D: All of the reasons given are good ones for locating the camps near the source of food production.

22. J: As the human population increased, they depleted many of their food source faster than the populations could reproduce and renew themselves.

23. D: The moa were flightless birds, so they could not easily escape when the humans came to hunt them.

24. F: The Maori turned to cannibalism after the moa disappeared and they had lost a major source of food and protein.

Humanities

25. D: The passage describes the artistry of Greek coinage and gives the reasons why so much effort went into designing them.

26. G: The first sentence shows that the author thinks of coins as utilitarian objects and that few of them are designed in a manner that makes them worth considering as something more than that.

27. A: "Delectation" means to savor or to enjoy the flavor or beauty of something, in this case the design of the coins.

28. J: The word is defined in passing in the text in the second sentence.

29. D: The passage describes the coins as artistic objects, not simply because they were the first coins, but also because of the historical situation which is described, and which led to their being designed with great care and pride.

30. H: The text states that new coins were developed frequently, to commemorate battles, treaties, etc.

ScienceTest

PART A
1. D: The table shows that the lambda particle has a mass of over 1115 MeV All the other choices have less mass.

2. H: Protons and other nucleons are baryons, which are made of quarks. The other choices are all leptons, which are not.

3. D: To satisfy the law of conservation of charge, the net charge of allthe particles produced in a decay must equal that of the original particle. Note that while conservation of mass applies to the decay, it does not pertain to charge.

4. J: The most massive particles of neutral charge are the Xi particles, with a mass of 1314.9 MeV.

5. A: The lambda particle has no charge. The proton has a charge of +1. To satisfy the law of conservation of charge, the other particle must have a charge of -1. The negative pion is the only

choice that satisfies that condition.

6. H: The mass of the muon is 105.65 MeV. That of the positron is 0.65 MeV. To satisfy the law of conservation of mass, the mass of the positron plus that of the other resulting particles cannot add up to more than 105.65 MeV. Among the choices given, only the neutrino is small enough to satisfy that condition.

7. A: To satisfy the law of conservation of mass, the mass difference between the original particle and its decay products is released as knetic energy. Since the omega particle has a mass of 1672.45 MeV, and the kaon and lambda particles have masses of 493.68 and 1115.68 MeV, respectively, the difference is 63.09 MeV.

8. G: One MeV is equivalent to 1.783×10^{-30} kilogram, so that $60\,kg = \dfrac{60}{1.783 \times 10^{-30}}$ MeV = 33.65×10^{30} MeV.

PART B

9. B: An allele is a variant of the original DNA sequence for a gene. It may differ from the original by a single base (for example, it may contain a C in place of a G), or by a whole region in which the sequence of bases differ. It may have extra bases in it (insertions) or be missing some material (deletions). Whatever the difference, it will result in RNA, and subsequently a protein, whose sequence differs from that of the original. Sometimes, these differing proteins are defective. They may result in disease or developmental anomalies. Sometimes they are benign, as in the difference between blue and brown eyes in humans.

10. F: The sequence can be read directly from the table. It is read three bases at a time, since three bases constitute a codon and provide the information required to specify a single amino acid. In the sequence given, the first codon is GTT. The table shows that this corresponds to the amino acid valine. Similarly, the second codon is ACA, which corresponds to threonine. The third codon, AAA, corresponds to lysine, and the fourth, AGA, to arginine. Each sequence of amino acids produces a specific protein which is different from any other.

11. D: Begin parsing each sequence from the first base and break it into triplets to represent each codon. The sequence in choice A, for example, is GTA CCC CTA, representing valine-proline-leucine. Only the sequence in choice D contains one of the three STOP codons, which are TGA, TAA, and TAG. In choice D, the second codon is TAA. When the polymerase reaches this codon, it will begin the process of disengaging from the DNA, ending the mRNA copy and ultimately the protein product of the gene.

12. F: The DNA molecule is a long chain of phosphoribose to which bases are attached. The sequence of bases specifies the individual amino acids that are chained together to make a protein. There are 4 different bases and 23 different amino acids. Each amino acid is specified by a three-base "word," called a codon in the language of DNA. As the table shows, the 4 bases can be strung together in 64 different ways to encode the 23 different amino acids (plus STOP signals), so that some amino acids may be specified by more than a single codon.

13. C: While proteins are *encoded* in the DNA, they are actually *produced* by ribosomes, which string the proteins together from amino acids in the cell's cytoplasm. The information required to string

proteins into the correct sequence is provided by mRNAs that are made by polymerases, which read the codons in the DNA. Transfer RNAs bring the amino acids to the ribosomes, where they are assembled into proteins.

14. J: Phosphoribose provides the backbone of the DNA chain of which genes are comprised. There, bases such as cytosine and guanine are strung together and organized into triplets known as codons, which encode the protein to be made. The protein itself will be assembled far from the gene, which is in the cell's nucleus, by the ribosome, which is in the cytoplasm of the cell.

PART C
15. A: The reactions described in the text are ones during which negatively charged electrons are produced by a reaction that reduces the positively-charged lead anode. The reducing agent, in turn, is oxidized by this reaction. These electrons travel through the wire to the negatively-charged cathode, where they react with the sulfuric acid oxidizer and reduce it, forming lead sulfate. In a car battery, the anode is the positively-charged electrode, and is normally indicated by a red marking.

16. F: In an oxidation reaction, an oxidizing agent gains electrons from a reducing agent. By contributing electrons, the reducing agent reduces (makes more negative) the charge on the oxidizer. In the car battery, reduction of the positively-charged anode provides electrons, which then flow to the cathode, where an oxidation takes place. In an oxidation, an oxidizing agent increases (makes more positive) the charge on a reducer. In this way, the extra electrons in the negatively charged cathode are neutralized by the surrounding oxidizing agent.

17. D: The reaction described in the text is one during which two water molecules (H_2O) are produced for each lead oxide (PbO_2) molecule that reacts at the cathode.

PART D
18. J: The term *hydrologic cycle* is defined in the first paragraph, where it is described as being equivalent to the *water cycle*. It is derived from the Greek root *hydros*, which means "water."

19. B: The second paragraph gives examples of different storage reservoirs for water in the water cycle. Underground aquifers are one of the examples given. An *aquifer* (a word derived from the Latin root *aqua*, meaning water) is any geologic formation containing ground water.

20. J: According to the table, the average residence time of water in soil is only two months. Only its residence time in the atmosphere, 9 days, is shorter. *Residence time* is defined in the text as the average amount of time that a water molecule spends in each of the reservoirs shown in the table before it moves on to the next reservoir of the water cycle.

21. B: According to the final paragraph of the text, ocean levels actually fall during an ice age. This is because more water is stored in ice caps and glaciers when the prevailing temperatures are very cold, so less water remains in the oceans.

PART E
22. H: Because the addition of heat causes the molecules of a substance to increase their rate of motion, it is considered a form of kinetic energy. The temperature of a substance is proportional to the kinetic energy of the molecules of which it is made. Addition of heat to a system usually results in an increase in temperature, but temperature is not a form of heat. It is a measure of the amount of kinetic energy present in a system.

23. C: Energy in the form of heat is always absorbed by the molecules of a substance to make them move faster. During a change of state, some molecules are absorbing energy and escaping the solid phase to become liquid, or escaping the liquid phase to become gas. Since molecules in a gas move faster than those in a liquid and molecules in a liquid move faster than those in a gas, the average speed increases. Note that choice E is incorrect since the heat of vaporization for water is greater than its heat of fusion.

24. J: In region B of the graph, the water is at 0°C. Heat is being added to it and it is progressively changing to a liquid. In region C, the temperature is climbing from 0°C to 100°C, and all of the water is in a liquid phase. In region D, the water is at 100°C, and is progressively changing to a gas as more energy is added. Once it has all changed to a gas, the temperature will once again increase as more heat is added (region E).

25. D: Water at 1°C is in the liquid phase. Using the definition of the specific heat capacity given in the text, it will take 99 calories to raise the temperature of 1 gm of liquid water to 100°C. Using the definition of the heat of vaporization given in the text, it will take an additional 540 calories to turn it into the gaseous phase once it reaches 100°C. Finally, an additional calorie must be added to bring the temperature of the gas up to 101°C. Therefore, the total amount of heat which must be added is 640 calories.

26. G: Region B of the graph represents the transition between the solid and liquid phases of water. If heat is added to the system, solid water melts into liquid. Conversely, if heat is removed from the system, liquid water will freeze in this region of the graph. Similarly, region D represents the transition between liquid and gaseous water. In this region, water either evaporates or condenses, depending upon whether heat is added to or removed from it.

PART F
27. C: The axon is the sending extension of the neuron or nerve cell. A terminal is the end of an axon. A dendrite is the receiving extension of the neuron. A synapse is the gap between the terminal of one neuron's axon and the dendrite of another neuron, wherein electrochemical reactions take place to continue message transmission by exciting the membrane of the next cell in the chain.

28. G: The dendrite is the receiving extension of the neuron or nerve cell. It receives messages from the axon, or sending extension, of another neuron. The place between cells, where they release chemical neurotransmitters to transmit information from neuron to neuron, is a synapse. A terminal is the end of an axon.

29. A: The space or gap where nerve cells, or neurons, emit chemical neurotransmitters to communicate messages to other neurons is a synapse. Neurons send information in the form of electrical impulses via their axons, or sending extensions, to the dendrites, or receiving extensions, of other neurons. The end of a neuron's axon is its terminal.

30. G: Glial cells, also known as "white matter" to distinguish them from the brain's "gray matter" or cortex, produce myelin, which coats the neurons to protect them and facilitate communication among them. Cell membranes of neurons are excited by chemicals called neurotransmitters emitted by neighboring neurons, creating electrical reactions to further the chain of message transmission. Cell bodies are the small centers of neurons, while their axons and dendrites are extensions for sending and receiving messages. Synapses are the gaps between adjacent cells where electrochemical reactions occur to transmit information from cell to cell.

Practice Test #2

Practice Questions

English Test

Questions 1 – 15 pertain to the following passage:

<u>Passage I</u>

The Wampanoag Indians of the Northeast were typical of the tribes of the time. They (1)<u>speak</u> a language that is a part of the Algonquin language family. At that time, the Wampanoag people lived (2)<u>in what is Massachusetts</u>. (3)<u>Today, the descendants</u> of these Indians speak English and live in southern Massachusetts and Rhode Island.

The Wampanoag religion was similar to that of the other Algonquin tribes. In those bygone times, the people believed in a Great Spirit (4)<u>and also</u> that all things in Nature had a part of the Great Spirit in them. They also had spiritual beliefs (5)<u>about animals, and the</u> forest. They expressed their religious beliefs during festivals and at night, when they sat together at huge campfires. Then, they told (6)<u>their</u> stories of the cycle of life (7)<u>and the</u> Great Spirit. Now, (8)<u>some Indians that are a part of the Wampanoags</u> still worship in the traditional (9)<u>way but many</u> have adopted western religions.

The Wampanoag diet consisted mostly of fish and other (10)<u>animals, they</u> also ate (11)<u>corn, and beans, and squash</u>. The Wampanoag hunters ranged far and wide, from land to (12)<u>the</u> sea. They trapped small animals and caught shellfish, including crabs and lobsters. (13)<u>Besides animals,</u> they grew fruits and vegetables. To survive the winter, they were able to preserve a lot of this food (14)<u>and eat it</u>.

The Wampanoag lived in houses (15)<u>called a *wetu*</u>. A *wetu* is a round building with a round roof. The men of the tribe were responsible for constructing the *wetu*. They made the dwelling by tying sticks and branches together, and then putting grass and tree bark on top to make the roof. The Wampanoag also built long houses, which were much larger and were used for tribal meetings.

1. A. NO CHANGE
   B. spoke
   C. understand
   D. speaks

2. F. NO CHANGE
   G. in what is now Massachusetts
   H. in
   J. in Massachusetts now

3. A. NO CHANGE
   B. Recent descendants
   C. Today the descendants
   D. Current descendants

4. F. and, also
   G. and
   H. also
   J. NO CHANGE

5. A. NO CHANGE
   B. about animals, and about the
   C. about animals and the
   D. and the

6. F. NO CHANGE
   G. there
   H. they're
   J. sitting

7. A. NO CHANGE
   B. of the
   C. and of the
   D. and, of the

8. F. NO CHANGE
   G. some Wampanoags
   H. some Indians
   J. some Indians that are Wampanoags

9. A. NO CHANGE
   B. way, but many
   C. way, but, many
   D. way, many

10. F. NO CHANGE
    G. animals, and they also
    H. animals, also
    J. animals. They also

11. A. NO CHANGE
    B. corn, and beans and squash
    C. corn, beans, and squash
    D. corn beans and squash

12. F. NO CHANGE
    G. near the
    H. over
    J. OMIT THIS WORD

13. A. NO CHANGE
    B. Besides hunting
    C. Besides, hunting
    D. Other than animals,

14. F. NO CHANGE
    G. OMIT THIS PHRASE
    H. while eating it
    J. while they ate it

15. A. NO CHANGE
    B. called wetu
    C. or wetu
    D. in wetu

Questions 16 – 30 pertain to the following passage:
Passage II

Once upon a time, (16)there was a village in the jungle, a man appeared and announced to the villagers that he would buy monkeys for $10 each.

(17)Seeing as how there were many monkeys around, the villagers went out to the (18)forest, and started catching them. The man bought thousands at $10, (19)and, as the supply started to diminish, the villagers let (20)there efforts lag. The man (21)later announced that he would buy monkeys at $20 each. This renewed the vigor of the (22)villagers and got them catching monkeys again.

Soon the supply diminished even further, and people started going back to their farms. The offer was increased, this time to $25 each, and the supply of monkeys became so (23)few that it was an effort (24)to even see a monkey, (25)let alone catch one!

Well, the man now decided to raise his price (26)again he announced that he would buy monkeys at $50! However, since he had to go to the city on some business, he introduced the villagers to his assistant. "My assistant's name is Eddie. Here he is. (27)This is him. While I am away, Eddie will be the one who buys the monkeys, (28)not me."

With the man gone, Eddie (29)tells the villagers, "Look, I have a great idea. Look at all these monkeys in the big cage that the man has collected. I will sell them to you at $35 and when he gets back from the city, you can easily sell them to him for $50 each."

The villagers all thought this was an excellent idea. They collected their savings,

- 43 -

rounded up all the money they could find, and proceeded to buy back all of the monkeys. Eddie took their money and disappeared into the forest. The villagers waited for the first man to return from the city, so they could sell him the monkeys for $50, but he never came. They never again saw him or his assistant, Eddie, (30)<u>only monkeys everywhere</u>!

16. F. NO CHANGE
    G. there was once
    H. in
    J. there is

17. A. NO CHANGE
    B. Since
    C. Seeing that
    D. Noticing that

18. F. NO CHANGE
    G. forest and
    H. woods, and
    J. skillfully

19. A. NO CHANGE
    B. since
    C. when
    D. but

20. F. NO CHANGE
    G. OMIT this word
    H. they're
    J. their

21. A. NO CHANGE
    B. OMIT this word
    C. soon
    D. kindly

22. F. NO CHANGE
    G. villagers though
    H. townspeople, and
    J. villagers, and

23. A. NO CHANGE
    B. OMIT this word
    C. limited
    D. distracted

- 44 -

24. F. NO CHANGE
   G. even to see
   H. to see even
   J. to see

25. A. NO CHANGE
   B. not only catch one
   C. let alone to catch one
   D. if only to catch one

26. F. NO CHANGE
   G. again; he announced
   H. again, he announced
   J. again...he announced

27. A. NO CHANGE
   B. This is Eddie.
   C. This is Ed.
       D. This is he.

28. F. NO CHANGE
   G. not I
   H. despite me
   J. with me

29. A. NO CHANGE
   B. speaks to
   C. told
   D. went to

30. F. NO CHANGE
   G. instead of them they saw monkeys
   H. because of the monkeys
   J. so they looked at the monkeys

Questions 31 – 40 pertain to the following passage:
Passage III

   The staff of the group home (31) were taking the residents on (32) a outing. Jacques
   was (33) suppose (34) to also go on the trip with them. Driving up the street, (35)
   the group home van was not parked in front of the house. When he got (36) their,
   Jacques found out they (37) had already went on (38) they're trip to the lake
   without him. In our (39) specialists' supervision meeting with our supervisor, Sarah,
   and Theresa and (40) I, he reported this event.

31 A. NO CHANGE
   B. was taking
   C. took
   D. takes

- 45 -

32 F. NO CHANGE
    G. the
    H. an
    J. and

33. A. NO CHANGE
    B. supposing
    C. supposed
    D. supposedly

34. F. NO CHANGE
    G. to go also on the trip with them
    H. to go on the trip also with them
    J. to go on the trip with them also

35. A. NO CHANGE
    B. Driving up the street, Jacques saw that the group home van...
    C. Driving up the street, the group home van was not seen by Jacques...
    D. Jacques did not see the group home van driving up the street

36. F. NO CHANGE
    G. they're
    H. there
    J. theyre

37. A. NO CHANGE
    B. Were already going
    C. Are already gone
    D. Had already gone

38. F. NO CHANGE
    G. their
    H. they're
    J. they

39. A. NO CHANGE
    B. specialist's
    C. specialists
    D. specialist

40. F. NO CHANGE
    G. me
    H. we
    J. them

Mathematics Test

1. Find the sum.

$(3x^2 + x + 3) + 8x^2 + 5x + 16$

    A. $7x^2 + 29\ x^2$

    B. $11x^2 + 6x + 19$

    C. $30x + 19$

    D. $(3x^2 + 3x) + 13x^2 + 16$

    E. $36x^2$

2. A wall clock has the numbers 1 through 12 written on it. If you spin the second hand, what is the probability of landing on an even number?

    F. 20%

    G. 30%

    H. 40%

    J. 50%

    K. 100%

3. What is the perimeter of the following figure?

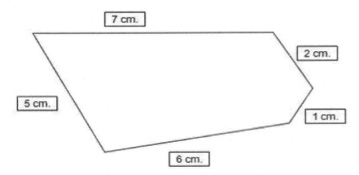

    A. 15cm

    B. 18cm

    C. 21 cm

    D. 36cm

    E. 45cm

4. Angle AEC is a straight line. Angle BEC is 45°. What is the measure for angle AEB?

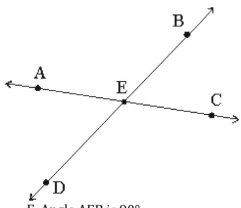

F. Angle AEB is 90°
G. Angle AEB is 115°
H. Angle AEB is 135°
J. Angle AEB is 180°
K. Angle AEB is 360°

Use the figure below to answer questions 5, 6, and 7.

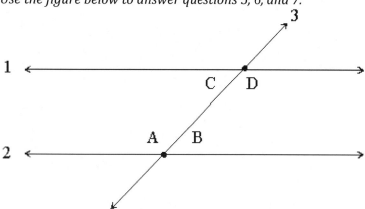

5. Which of the following statements is true about the figure above?
   A. Lines 1 and 2 are parallel.
   B. Lines 1 and 3 are parallel.
   C. Lines 1 and 2 intersect.
   D. Line 1 bisects line 3.
   E. Line 2 corresponds with angle B.

6. In the figure above, which of the following is a pair of alternate interior angles?
   F. angle C and angle D
   G. angle A and angle B
   H. angle A and angle C
   J. angle B and angle D
   K. angle A and angle D

- 48 -

7. In the figure above, which of the following is an obtuse angle?
   A. line 1
   B. line 2
   C. line 3
   D. angle A
   E. angle B

8. To begin making her soup, Jennifer added four containers of chicken broth with 1 liter of water into the pot. Each container of chicken broth contains 410 milliliters. How much liquid is in the pot?
   F. 1.64 liters
   G. 2.64 liters
   H. 5.44 liters
   J. 6.12 liters
   K. 17.4 liters

9. What are the first 5 multiples of 8?
   A. 1, 2, 3, 4, 5
   B. 0, 2, 4, 6, 8
   C. 0, 8, 16, 24, 32
   D. 1, 8, 16, 24, 32
   E. 8, 16, 24, 32, 40

10. Which of the following demonstrates 25,125,652 in scientific notation?
   F. $2,512,565.2 \times 10$
   G. 251256.52×10^2
   H. $25,125.652 \times 10^3$
   J. 25.125652×10^6
   K. 2.5125652×10^7

11. What is 44/99 in the simplest form?
   A. 4/9
   B. 4/5
   C. 11/99
   D. 14/19
   E. 44/99

12. According to the table below, which snack is made with no more than 4 grams of sugar and between 4-6 grams of carbohydrates?

Snack (amount per serving)	Grams of Sugar per Serving	Grams of Carbohydrates per Serving
Snappy Cookies (3)	6	8
Snappy Crackers (8)	6	4
Snappy Cheese (2)	0	0
Snappy Twisters (4)	4	5
Snappy Chews (20)	0	8

   F. Snappy Cookies
   G. Snappy Crackers
   H. Snappy Cheese
   J. Snappy Twisters
   K. Snappy Chews

13. Which of the following is an example of a ray?

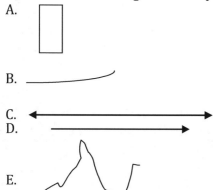

14. All of the children are girls. Some of the girls like soccer. Some of the girls like cheerleading. Based on this data, which statement has to be correct?

    F. All girls like to play soccer.
    G. Some of the girls are 3 years old.
    H. Some of the girls like both soccer and cheerleading.
    J. Some of the children like soccer.
    K. Some of the girls do not like soccer or cheerleading.

15. Which of the following fractions is halfway between 2/5 and 4/9?

    A. 2/3
    B. 2/20
    C. 17/40
    D. 19/45
    E. 20/45

16. Fifteen ring boxes can fit into each case. If you have 100 ring boxes, how many cases do you need?

    F. 4 cases
    G. 5 cases
    H. 6 cases
    J. 7 cases
    K. 8 cases

17. Which of the following is the largest number?

    A. 1/2
    B. 3/8
    C. 7/16
    D. 13/54
    E. 89/287

18. Which number has no remainder when divided into 250?

    F. 5

    G. 15

    H. 20

    J. 30

    K. 75

19. If the average of 7 and x is equal to the average of 9, 4, and x, what is the value of x?

    A. 4

    B. 5

    C. 6

    D. 7

    E. 8

20. If four friends had an average score of 92 on a test, what was Annie's score if Bill got an 86, Clive got a 98 and Demetrius got a 90?

    F. 88

    G. 90

    H. 92

    J. 94

    K. 96

21. If $3x - 2 = 1$, then $x =$

    A. 4

    B. 3

    C. 2

    D. 1

    E. -1

22. If $2^4 = 4^x$, then $x =$

    F. 2

    G. 4

    H. 6

    J. 8

    K. 10

23. If $2x + 3y = 13$ and $4x - y = 5$, then $3x + 2y =$

    A. 2

    B. 3

    C. 6

    D. 12

    E. 24

24. If x is a positive integer, then 30% of 2x equals

    F. x

    G. x/5

    H. 2x/5

    J. 3x/5

    K. 4x/5

25. How many integers are solutions of the inequality |x| < 4?
  A. An infinite number
  B. 0
  C. 3
  D. 6
  E. 7

26. What is the value of (-5) + (-3)?
  F. -2
  G. 2
  H. -1
  J. -8
  K. 8

27. A rectangle is divided into two squares, each with a perimeter of 20. What is the perimeter of the rectangle?
  A. 20
  B. 30
  C. 40
  D. 50
  E. 60

Questions 28-30 pertain to the following table:

Top Three Majors at Greenly Community College

	Percentage of Class in Major		
	History	Engineering	Spanish
Freshmen	30	25	17
Sophomore	33	21	18
Junior	36	22	14
Senior	29	28	19

28. What percentage of freshmen are studying a major other than history, engineering or Spanish?
  F. 8%
  G. 18%
  H. 28%
  J. 38%
  K. 48%

29. If class sizes are the same for all 4 years, what percentage of the overall student body is studying history?
  A. 29
  B. 30
  C. 31
  D. 32
  E. 33

30. Which of the following are the lowest terms for expressing the ratio of the percentage of juniors majoring in Spanish to the percentage of juniors majoring in history?

    F. 14 : 36

    G. 14 : 22

    H. 7 : 11

    J. 7 : 18

    K. 14 : 18

Reading Test

Questions 1 – 10 pertain to the following Prose Fiction passage:

AMERICAN LITERATURE – SHORT STORY

In the enthusiasm of my confidence, I brought chairs into the room, and desired them here to rest from their fatigues, while I myself, in the wild audacity of my perfect triumph, placed my own seat upon the very spot beneath which reposed the corpse of the victim.

The officers were satisfied. My manner had convinced them. I was singularly at ease. They sat, and while I answered cheerily, they chatted of familiar things. But, ere long, I felt myself getting pale and wished them gone. My head ached, and I fancied a ringing in my ears: but still they sat and still chatted. The ringing became more distinct: --It continued and became more distinct: I talked more freely to get rid of the feeling: but it continued and gained definiteness --until, at length, I found that the noise was not within my ears.

No doubt I now grew very pale; --but I talked more fluently, and with a heightened voice. Yet the sound increased --and what could I do? It was a low, dull, quick sound --much such a sound as a watch makes when enveloped in cotton. I gasped for breath --and yet the officers heard it not. I talked more quickly --more vehemently; but the noise steadily increased. I arose and argued about trifles, in a high key and with violent gesticulations; but the noise steadily increased. Why would they not be gone? I paced the floor to and fro with heavy strides, as if excited to fury by the observations of the men --but the noise steadily increased. Oh God! what could I do? I foamed --I raved --I swore! I swung the chair upon which I had been sitting, and grated it upon the boards, but the noise arose over all and continually increased. It grew louder --louder --louder! And still the men chatted pleasantly, and smiled. Was it possible they heard not? Almighty God! --no, no! They heard! --they suspected! --they knew! --they were making a mockery of my horror!-this I thought, and this I think. But anything was better than this agony! Anything was more tolerable than this derision! I could bear those hypocritical smiles no longer! I felt that I must scream or die! and now --again! --hark! louder! louder! louder! louder!

"Villains!" I shrieked, "dissemble no more! I admit the deed! --tear up the planks! here, here! --It is the beating of his hideous heart!"

-THE END-

--From "The Tell-Tale Heart" by Edgar Allan Poe, 1843

1. In the second paragraph, why is the narrator "singularly at ease"?
    A. Because he has not committed any crime
    B. Because the officers are just visiting and chatting
    C. Because he has convinced the officers of his innocence
    D. Because he feels only pride at what he has accomplished

2. Why does the narrator say he found himself "getting pale and wished them gone"?
    F. They have overstayed their welcome
    G. Their conversation is annoying to him
    H. He has been working for a long time
    J. He secretly fears discovery of his act

3. What does "My head ached, and I fancied a ringing in my ears" signify?
    A. The narrator is suffering from a physiological condition
    B. The narrator is suffering from psychological symptoms
    C. The narrator cannot tolerate the officers' conversation
    D. The narrator was subjected to prolonged interrogation

4. The narrator states that "...at length, I found that the noise was not within my ears." What does this mean?
    F. The noise was in the room where they were sitting
    G. The noise was outside of the building in the street
    H. The noise was coming from under the floorboards
    J. The noise was from the narrator's own heartbeat

5. The narrator states that he placed his chair in the spot above the victim's corpse. Which is true?
    A. The victim was murdered by the narrator
    B. The victim was killed by another person
    C. The narrator only imagines the corpse
    D. The officers are aware of the corpse

6. The narrator says, "I paced the floor to and fro with heavy strides, as if excited to fury by the observations of the men..." Which of the following is most true about this description?
    F. He was actually infuriated by the observations the officers were making
    G. He was doing this in an attempt to keep the men from hearing the noise
    H. He was faking being excited to distract the men from their observations
    J. He was "excited to fury" by the obvious suspicions of the police officers

7. "I foamed --I raved --I swore!" Related to this description (third paragraph) of his actions by the story's narrator, which is most correct?
    A. The only reason he did these things was because he was clearly insane
    B. He did these things because the police's questions made him agitated
    C. He was behaving this way primarily to drive the police officers to leave
    D. He was desperately trying to distract the police from hearing the noise

8. "And still the men chatted pleasantly, and smiled. Was it possible they heard not? Almighty God! --no, no! They heard! --they suspected! --they knew! --they were making a mockery of my horror!-- this I thought, and this I think." Regarding this, which of the following is most accurate?

    E. The men knew nothing at first, then suspected, and then knew, but were not mocking him

    F. The men knew nothing, then suspected, then knew, and were mocking him just as he says

    G. The men knew and suspected nothing and were not mocking him; he only imagined these

    J. The men knew from the beginning of the narrator's guilt and were pretending they didn't

9. Appropriately to its content, in this story Poe's writing style is characterized most by the literary technique of:

    A. repetition

    B. elaboration

    C. great detail

    D. wordiness

10. Regarding the narrator's confession in the final paragraph/sentence, which of the following is true?

    E. He had unwittingly buried the victim alive, and his heart could still be heard beating

    F. He had mistaken his own increasingly loud heartbeat for the heartbeat of the victim

    G. He had become obsessed with lingering memories of the sound of the victim's heart

    J. He had begun to imagine hearing the victim's heart beating, but really heard nothing

Questions 11 – 20 pertain to the following Social Sciences passage:

PSYCHOLOGY

It is easy to show that the wish-fulfilment in dreams is often undisguised and easy to recognize, so that one may wonder why the language of dreams has not long since been understood. There is, for example, a dream which I can evoke as often as I please, experimentally, as it were. If, in the evening, I eat anchovies, olives, or other strongly salted foods, I am thirsty at night, and therefore I wake. The waking, however, is preceded by a dream, which has always the same content, namely, that I am drinking. I am drinking long draughts of water; it tastes as delicious as only a cool drink can taste when one's throat is parched; and then I wake, and find that I have an actual desire to drink. The cause of this dream is thirst, which I perceive when I wake. From this sensation arises the wish to drink, and the dream shows me this wish as fulfilled. It thereby serves a function, the nature of which I soon surmise. I sleep well, and am not accustomed to being waked by a bodily need. If I succeed in appeasing my thirst by means of the dream that I am drinking, I need not wake up in order to satisfy that thirst. It is thus a dream of convenience. The dream takes the place of action, as elsewhere in life. Unfortunately, the need of water to quench the thirst cannot be satisfied by a dream, as can my thirst for revenge upon Otto and Dr. M, but the intention is the same. Not long ago I had the same dream in a somewhat modified form. On this occasion I felt thirsty before going to bed, and emptied the glass of water which stood on the little chest beside my bed. Some hours later, during the night, my thirst returned, with the consequent discomfort. In order to obtain water, I should have had to get up and fetch the glass which stood on my wife's bed-table. I thus quite appropriately dreamt that my wife was giving me a drink from a vase; this vase was an Etruscan cinerary urn, which I had brought home from Italy and had since given away. But the water in it tasted so salt (apparently on account of the ashes) that I was forced to wake. It may be observed

- 55 -

how conveniently the dream is capable of arranging matters. Since the fulfilment of a wish is its only purpose, it may be perfectly egoistic. Love of comfort is really not compatible with consideration for others. The introduction of the cinerary urn is probably once again the fulfilment of a wish; I regret that I no longer possess this vase; it, like the glass of water at my wife's side, is inaccessible to me. The cinerary urn is appropriate also in connection with the sensation of an increasingly salty taste, which I know will compel me to wake.

--From The Dream as Wish-Fulfilment in The Interpretation of Dreams, 3rd Edition by Sigmund Freud, translated by A. A. Brill, 1911

11. What does Freud mean by "wish-fulfilment" in dreams?
    A. Some dreams meet a real need in the mind rather than in reality
    B. Having a dream can make wishes come true that actions cannot
    C. Fulfilling a wish in a dream eliminates the need to wake and act
    D. Dreaming of getting your wish will never satisfy you when awake

12. When he writes of "a dream which I can evoke as often as I please," what does the author mean?
    F. He can erase it from his memory
    G. He can cause the dream to recur
    H. He can describe it when awake
    J. He can remember it completely

13. What does Freud say is a need that he can satisfy simply by dreaming about it?
    A. The need to eat a salty food
    B. The need to quench his thirst
    C. The need to exact his revenge
    D. The need to awaken himself

14. Why does Freud surmise that the water from the urn in his dream tasted salty because of ashes?
    F. He really dreamed it was salty because he was thirsty
    G. The vase was a cinerary urn used to empty fireplaces
    H. The vase was a cinerary urn for collecting oven cinders
    J. The vase was a cinerary urn for holding cremation ash

15. What does the author remark about his being awakened by thirst?
    A. He states that this is a phenomenon that he experiences frequently
    B. He finds that his thirst need not awaken him if he dreams of drinking
    C. He states that he only wakes up from thirst when he is not dreaming
    D. He states he is not used to waking up that often from physical needs

16. What happened to the Etruscan urn from Italy that Freud dreamt of and describes?
    F. It never existed except in his dream
    G. It appears that he may have lost it
    H. He broke it after bringing it home
    J. He gave it away after obtaining it

17. What is one way that the vase Freud dreamed of drinking from is associated with his wife?
   A. This vase or urn actually belonged to his wife
   B. His wife had brought the vase back from Italy
   C. He dreamed of her giving him a drink from it
   D. The vase was located on his wife's bed-table

18. When he wrote that wish fulfillment could be "perfectly egoistic," Freud meant that it could be
   F. truthful
   G. selfish
   H. realistic
   J. heroic

19. Why did Freud describe both his wife's water glass and the cinerary urn as "inaccessible" to him?
   A. He could not reach the glass while in bed and he no longer had the urn
   B. Both the glass and the urn were in the bedroom but were out of reach
   C. He could not reach the urn from bed and his wife's glass was not there
   D. Both his wife's water glass and the cinerary urn were no longer present

20. Which is correct regarding the points Freud makes about dreams as wish-fulfillment in this passage?
   F. Wish-fulfillment dreams always eliminate the need for action by meeting a need
   G. Dreaming about satisfying a psychological need like getting revenge is ineffective
   H. Dreaming about satisfying a physical need like thirst replaces really drinking water
   J. Having a wish-fulfillment dream actually serves a purpose and performs a function

Questions 21 – 30 pertain to the following Humanities passage:
RELIGION, PHILOSOPHY

I conclude therefore and say, there is no happinesse under (or as *Copernicus* will have it, above) the Sunne, nor any Crambe in that repeated veritie and burthen of all the wisedom of *Solomon, All is vanitie and vexation of spirit;* there is no felicity in that the world adores. *Aristotle* whilst hee labours to refute the Idea's of *Plato,* fals upon one himselfe: for his *summum bonum* is a *Chimaera,* and there is no such thing as his Felicity. That wherein God himself is happy, the holy Angels are happy, in whose defect the Devils are unhappy; that dare I call happinesse: whatsoever conduceth unto this, may with an easie Metaphor deserve that name; whatsoever else the world termes happines, is to me a story out of *Pliny,* an apparition, or neat delusion, wherein there is no more of happinesse than the name. Blesse mee in this life with but the peace of my conscience, command of my affections, the love of thy selfe and my dearest friends, and I shall be happy enough to pity *Caesar.* These are O Lord the humble desires of my most reasonable ambition and all I dare call happinesse on earth: wherein I set no rule or limit to thy hand or providence. Dispose of me according to the wisedome of thy pleasure. Thy will bee done, though in my owne undoing.

FINIS.

--From *Religio Medici* (*The Religion of a Doctor*) by Sir Thomas Browne, 1643

21. The different spellings of many words in this passage are attributable to
    A. the fact that the author did not have an editor
    B. the author's individual spelling idiosyncrasies
    C. the status of the English language in the 1600s
    D. the author's coming from a different country

22. Which correctly explains Browne's reference to Copernicus in the first line?
    F. He was referring to Copernicus' grammatical correction from "under" to "above" the sun
    G. He was referring to Copernicus' challenging a geocentric universe with a heliocentric one
    H. He was referring to Copernicus' opinion about happiness as being different from his own
    J. He was referring to Copernicus' theory of the sun's movements with relation to the earth

23. What is true about the reference to Solomon and vanity in lines 2-3?
    A. Browne was using a quotation from the *Song of Solomon*
    B. Browne was describing Solomon's ideas in his own words
    C. Browne was quoting a Biblical scholar writing on Solomon
    D. Browne was quoting Solomon in the Bible book *Ecclesiastes*

24. What does the author mean most by "there is no felicity in that the world adores"?
    F. Worldly or material things that people covet do not bring them happiness
    G. Receiving the love or adoration of the world will not make a person happy
    H. All of the people in the world who experience love still do not attain grace
    J. People and things finding favor from the world are not necessarily happy

25. In Browne's reference to Aristotle, what is the *summum bonum*?
    A. It is Greek for "all of the bones."
    B. It means "the good of the many."
    C. It is Latin for "the best qualities."
    D. It is Latin for "the highest good."

26. What does the author mean most when he calls Aristotle's concept a "Chimaera"?
    F. He means that Aristotle's idea is a monster
    G. He means that Aristotle's idea is mythology
    H. He means that Aristotle's idea is not credible
    J. He means that Aristotle's idea does not exist

27. Browne states that what he dares to call happiness includes all these, EXCEPT
    A. anything that makes God happy
    B. things making the angels happy
    C. what makes the devils unhappy
    D. whatever makes people happy

28. Which of the following is NOT one of the blessings Browne asks in life in order to be happy?
    F. The peace of mind of having a clear conscience
    G. Having the ability to control his own emotions
    H. Experiencing the affection of his closest friends
    J. Receiving love for his desires and his ambitions

29. What does Browne mean when he writes "I shall be happy enough to pity Caesar"?
   A. He means that one must be totally happy in order to be able to pity others
   B. He means happiness so great that he would pity even the greatest success
   C. He means that a great emperor's power and wealth did not give happiness
   D. He means he will not be completely happy but at least happier than Caesar

30. What is the best interpretation of the closing sentence, "Thy will bee done, though in my owne undoing."?
   F. Browne believes that God's will takes precedence over his own individual human will
   G. Browne is saying that because of God's will, Browne's individual life has been ruined
   H. Browne is implying that God must ruin/undo Browne personally in order to do His will
   J. Browne is conveying that he must undo himself in order for God's will to be realized

Science Test

PART A

Questions 1 – 5 pertain to the following passage and diagram:

Are the messages ants send to one another visual, physical or chemical? Put a physical block (like a pebble) in their way. Can they make their way around it? Try disturbing them with noise. Then wash the surface carefully with window cleaner on a cotton swab to eliminate a chemical trail. Which kind of barrier confused their coordination?

SIGNALS, SENSES, AND SURVIVAL

Have you ever watched tiny animals, like ants, walk across a sidewalk? Even if individual ants can't see one another, they seem to "get the message" and follow one another to food. By responding to their environment in a coordinated way, ants survive and thrive by sending chemical messages to one another.

Even single-celled organisms can respond to environmental signals such as light, gravity, or chemicals. They can also coordinate their responses in a way that helps a group of organisms act together for their mutual advantage.

Studying how single-celled organisms communicate can help us understand how the cells within larger organisms might coordinate their responses. One experiment that explored this problem was done in 1883, by biologist Theodor Engelmann. He took a long strand of the green alga Spirogyra and spread it across a microscope slide.

Then he used a prism to create a spectrum (rainbow) of colors across the slide, so some parts of the alga got red light, some green, and some blue. Finally, he looked for tiny bacterial cells called E. coli in the water. These bacteria need oxygen to survive. He found that even the simplest bacterial cells could respond to chemical signals—and act together! They swarmed to the parts of the alga with the fastest rate of photosynthesis.

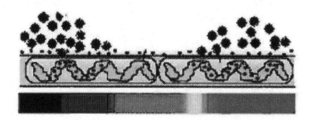

They could sense the chemical oxygen that the algal cells released, and move toward it in a coordinated way. (Bacteria move by twirling whip-like flagella.)

1. In the boxed instructions at the top for the ant experiment, what is the most likely answer to the question it poses based on the text that follows?
    A. The ants were confused by a visual barrier
    B. The ants were confused by a physical barrier
    C. The ants were confused by a chemical barrier
    D. The ants were confused by an auditory barrier

2. Engelmann conducted the referenced experiment in:
    F. the twentieth century
    G. the nineteenth century
    H. the eighteenth century
    J. the seventeenth century

3. Which of the following is NOT true of single-celled organisms according to this passage?
    A. They can respond to environmental light stimuli
    B. They can respond to environmental gravity stimuli
    C. They can respond to environmental chemical stimuli
    D. They can respond only as individual, separate organisms

4. In the context of this excerpt, Spirogyra is a(n):
    F. musical group
    G. bacterial cell
    H. spectrum
    J. alga

5. Which is correct regarding the organisms and photosynthesis as described in this passage?
    A. Algae use sunlight to produce food, emitting oxygen as waste, which bacteria need to live
    B. Bacteria use the oxygen that they get from algae to produce food, with sunlight as catalyst
    C. Both the algal and the bacterial organisms need both sunlight and oxygen for their survival
    D. Bacteria use the energy from sunlight to produce oxygen, which creates food for the algae

Questions 6 – 10 pertain to the following diagram and passage:

THE ARCHITECTURE OF THE BRAIN

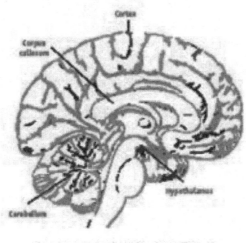

Image source: http://pubs.niaaa.nih.gov/
publications/arh284/images/tspart.gif

Biologists often compare the brains of many species of animals. There are many similarities across groups, but the relative proportions of each section provide important clues to the way the brain functions.

The most basic divisions of the brain are forebrain, midbrain, and hindbrain. The hindbrain is most like that of the simplest animals; it controls respiration and heart rate, and coordinates movement (the cerebellum). The amygdala is closely related to emotions. The hippocampus helps change short-term memories to longer memories.

The midbrain is the uppermost part of the brainstem, which controls reflexes and eye movement. In humans, the largest and most developed area is the forebrain. This includes the cerebrum.

The cerebrum is the largest part of the brain (85 percent by volume), with folds and wrinkles to increase its surface area. The corpus callosum connects the right and left hemisphere.

Each section of the cerebrum is specialized for specific function. Before the PET and MRI scan techniques came into common use, scientists could only probe cerebral functions during surgery or after accidents. Now we can look at the working brains of healthy people as they perform normal tasks. Here is a series of PET scans to show just a few of the revelations of these powerful new techniques.

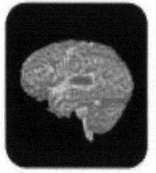 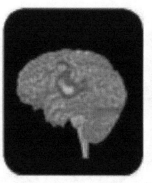 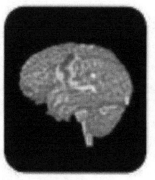 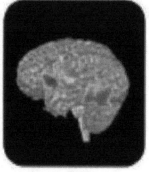

Hearing Words   Speaking Words   Seeing Words   Thinking about Words

6. Which part of the human brain is most similar to the brains of simpler animals?
    F. The front part
    G. The middle part
    H. The back part
    J. All of the parts

7. Which brain structure is involved in converting temporary memories to long-term storage?
    A. The hippocampus
    B. The hypothalamus
    C. The amygdala
    D. The cerebellum

8. The largest and most developed part of the brain in humans is the:
    F. corpus callosum
    G. cerebellum
    H. brainstem
    J. cerebrum

9. Based on the PET scans shown, performing which function shows the largest amounts of activity in different regions of the brain?
    A. Speaking words
    B. Hearing words
    C. Seeing words
    D. Thinking of words

10. Based on the PET scans shown, which brain function shows activity in the largest contiguous area?
    F. Hearing words
    G. Speaking words
    H. Seeing words
    J. Thinking about words

Questions 11 – 15 pertain to the following passage and diagram:

Introduction to Geologic Mapping

Geologic mapping is a highly interpretive, scientific process that can produce a range of map products for many different uses, including assessing ground-water quality and contamination risks; predicting earthquake, volcano, and landslide hazards; characterizing energy and mineral resources and their extraction costs; waste repository siting; land management and land-use planning; and general education. The value of geologic map information in public and private decision making (such as for the siting of landfills and highways) has repeatedly been described anecdotally, and has been demonstrated in benefit-cost analyses to reduce uncertainty and, by extension, potential costs.

The geologic mapper strives to understand the composition and structure of geologic materials at the Earth's surface and at depth, and to depict observations and interpretations on maps using symbols and colors (**Fig. 1**). Within the past 10 to 20 years, geographic information system (GIS) technology has begun to change some aspects of geologic mapping by providing software tools that permit the geometry and characteristics of rock bodies and other geologic features (such as faults) to be electronically stored, displayed, queried, and analyzed in conjunction with a seemingly infinite variety of other data types.

For example, GIS can be used to spatially compare possible pollutant sources (such as oil wells) with nearby streams and geologic units that serve as ground-water supplies. In addition, GIS can be used to compare the position of a proposed road with the surrounding geology to identify areas of high excavation costs or unstable slopes. These comparisons have always been possible, but GIS greatly facilitates the analysis and, as a result, offers geologists the opportunity to provide information in map form that is easily interpreted and used by the non-geologist.

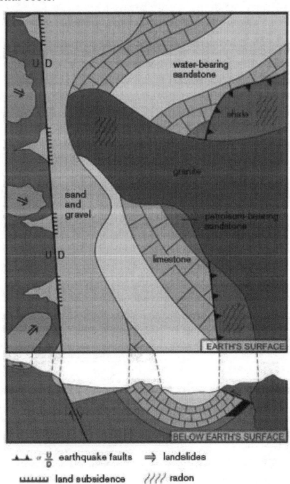

Figure 1. Graphic representation of typical information in a general purpose geologic map that can be used to identify geologic hazards, locate natural resources, and facilitate land-use planning. (After R. L. Bernknopf et al., 1993)

The public has come to expect near-instantaneous delivery of relevant, understandable information via the Internet, which in turn has begun to affect the methods used in geologic mapping, as well as the nature of the product. Geologists are rapidly incorporating GIS and information technology (IT) techniques into the production and dissemination of geologic maps...

--From the U.S. Geological Survey, 2005 (http://www.usgs.gov/)

11. According to this excerpt, which of these is true about the uses of geologic mapping?
    A. Geologic mapping cannot predict natural disasters such as mudslides or earthquakes
    B. Geologic mapping is an inappropriate method to locate landfills/other buried wastes
    C. Geologic mapping is unlikely to assess quality and/or contamination of ground water
    D. Geologic mapping can identify natural resources and estimate costs to acquire them

12. What is a significant change in geologic mapping that has occurred in recent years, according to the passage?
    F. Changes in the surface of the earth
    G. Changes in the bedrock of the earth
    H. Changes in the technology of the GIS
    J. Changes in the costs for excavations

13. On the sample map shown (Fig. 1), which type of rock is NOT present?
    A. Shale
    B. Basalt
    C. Granite
    D. Limestone

14. On the map shown in Fig. 1, where is radon gas located?
    F. In the petroleum-bearing sandstone
    G. In the water-bearing sandstone
    H. In the limestone and the shale
    J. In the shale and granite

15. Which of the following is identified on the Fig. 1 map by color rather than by symbol?
    A. Areas with specific types of rock
    B. Areas where landslides happen
    C. Fault lines causing earthquakes
    D. Areas where land has subsided

PART D

Questions 16 – 20 pertain to the following passage and diagram:

The Solar System

The words "solar system" refer to the Sun and all of the objects that travel around it. These objects include planets, natural satellites such as the Moon, the asteroid belt, comets, and meteoroids. Our solar system has an elliptical shape and is part of a galaxy known as the Milky Way. The Sun is the center of the solar system. It contains 99.8% of all of the mass in our solar system. Consequently, it exerts a tremendous gravitational pull on planets, satellites, asteroids, comets, and meteoroids. Astronomers believe the solar system formed 4.5 billion years ago. However, they differ in their beliefs about how the system formed. Some believe the whole solar system formed from a single flat cloud of gas, while others believe it formed when a huge object passed near the Sun, pulling a stream of gas off of the Sun. Astronomers theorize the planets then formed from this gas stream.

--From NASA, 2010

16. The Earth's Moon is a(n):
    F. meteoroid
    G. asteroid
    H. satellite
    J. comet

17. The shape of our solar system is:
    A. elliptical
    B. rectangular
    C. spherical
    D. spiral

18. How much of our solar system's total mass is held by the Sun?
    F. Half of it
    G. Two-thirds
    H. Four-fifths
    J. Almost all of it

19. The enormous gravitational pull of our Sun affects which of the following?
    A. Planets only
    B. Planets and satellites only
    C. Planets, satellites, and asteroids only
    D. Planets, satellites, asteroids, meteoroids, and comets

20. Current astronomers' theories mentioned in this passage include all BUT which component?
    F. All of the planets formed from one big flat cloud of gas
    G. All of the planets formed of meteor shower remnants
    H. A huge object pulled a stream of gas off from the Sun
    J. The planets formed from a stream of gas from the Sun

PART E

Questions 21 – 25 pertain to the following passage:
DEFINITION V: *A Centripetal force is that by which bodies are drawn or impelled, or any way tend, towards a point in the centre.*

Of this sort is Gravity by which bodies tend to the centre of the Earth; Magnetism, by which iron tends to the lodestone; and that force, whatever it is, by which the Planets are perpetually drawn aside from the rectilinear motions, which otherwise they would pursue, and made to revolve in curvilinear orbits. A stone, whirled about in a sling, endeavours to recede from the hand that turns it; and by that endeavour, distends the sling, and that with so much the greater force, as it is revolv'd with the greater velocity; and as soon as ever it is let go, flies away. That force which opposes it self to this endeavour, and by which the sling perpetually draws the stone towards the hand, and retains it in its orbit, because 'tis directed to the hand as the centre of the orbit, I call the Centripetal force. And the same thing is to be understood of all bodies, revolv'd in any orbits. They all endeavour to recede from the centres of their orbits; and were it not for the opposition of a contrary force which restrains them to, and detains them in their orbits, which I therefore call Centripetal, would fly off in right lines, with an uniform motion. A projectile, if it was not for the force of gravity, would not deviate towards the Earth, but would go off from it in a right line and that with an uniform motion, if the resistance of the Air was taken away. 'Tis by gravity that it is drawn aside perpetually from its rectilinear course, and made to deviate towards the Earth, more or less, according to the force of its gravity, and the velocity of its motion. The less its gravity is, for the quantity of its matter, or the greater the velocity with which it is projected, the less will it deviate from a rectilinear course, and the farther it will go. If a leaden ball projected from the top of a mountain by the force of gun-powder with a given velocity, and in a direction parallel to the horizon, is carried in a curve line to the distance of two miles before it falls to the ground; the same, if the resistance of the Air was took away, with a double or decuple velocity, would fly twice or ten times as far. And by increasing the velocity, we may at pleasure increase the distance to which it might be projected, and diminish the curvature of the line, which it might describe, till at last it should fall at the distance of 10, 30, or 90 degrees, or even might go quite round the whole Earth before it falls; or lastly, so that it might never fall to the Earth, but go forwards into the Celestial Spaces, and proceed in its motion *in infinitum.*

--From *The Mathematical Principles of Natural Philosophy* (*Philosophiæ Naturalis Principia Mathematica*) by Sir Isaac Newton, 1687, first English translation by John Machin, 1729

21. According to Newton, which is true about the motions of planets and other bodies?
    A. Without gravity, the planets would normally follow paths forming curving arcs
    B. Centripetal force causes objects to move away from the centers of their orbits
    C. Centripetal force is in opposition to the movements of objects in straight lines
    D. The magnetism of metals is an opposite force to the gravitational pull of Earth

22. In relation to the natural tendency of all circling bodies, Newton finds centripetal force is a(n)
    E. opposing force
    F. complementary force
    G. augmenting force
    J. supporting force

23. Based on this passage, if Earth's gravity were eliminated, what would a projectile do?
    A. It would fly straight up into the air
    B. It would fly outward in a straight line
    C. It would fall right down to the ground
    D. It would exhibit variable movements

24. Regarding Newton's example of a lead ball shot off a mountaintop, which of the following is correct if its velocity is increased?
    E. If its velocity is increased to twice as much, it will travel twice as far
    F. A tenfold increase in its velocity will cause it to go ten times farther
    G. The distance will increase ten times if projectile velocity is doubled
    J. Distance will increase equal to velocity if air resistance is removed

25. Newton speculated that if the speed of a projectile were increased enough, which of the following could happen?
    A. The line that it follows would become more curved
    B. It would fall at an angle which would stay constant
    C. It would always behave the same owing to gravity
    D. With enough speed, it could circumnavigate Earth

PART F

Director's Blog

In Search of the Missing Genetic Signals by Thomas Insel

Based on twin and family studies, we have long known that some mental disorders have a high degree of heritability, as great [as], or greater than most other common medical disorders. In recent years, NIMH-supported researchers have discovered several genes that are associated with autism spectrum disorder (ASD), schizophrenia, attention deficit hyperactivity disorder, and bipolar disorder. Most of these genes were discovered either through a candidate gene approach comparing cases and controls or by looking for linkage to genetic variation associated with occurrence of the disease in a family. However, the genomic variants discovered to date can explain only a small fraction of the genetic risk. So where are the missing genetic signals for mental disorders?

Three years ago, we thought the answer would come from whole genome association (WGA) studies. These studies were based on the identification of roughly 3 million points of common variation in the human genome. WGA studies used genotyping to measure hundreds of thousands of these single base differences between the genomes of those with and without a disorder. In what became known as the "common variant – common disease approach," genomic risk was mapped for a number of prevalent disorders, including macular degeneration, inflammatory bowel disease, and diabetes.[1] However, thus far, the search for common variations has yielded only a few success stories for mental disorders. These discoveries are notable, with potential implications for mechanisms of disease, but they still fall far short of explaining more than a small fraction of the genetic risk.

In the past two years, we have realized that people with serious mental disorders are more likely to have *rare* variations known as copy number variations (CNVs). CNVs are variations within the genome that result from deletions or duplications of genomic segments, sometimes involving millions of bases of DNA. CNVs are sometimes confined to a single family or develop "de novo" in just one individual. While each CNV is rare, there are so many of these structural variants (over 38,000 have been identified), that some scientists claim these CNVs contribute more variance than the millions of single base changes interrogated by WGA.[2] And unlike single base variations that usually have very modest effects on risk, some of these large mutations may be more penetrant, that is, more likely to cause disease.

Although these large CNVs are 10 times more common in people with schizophrenia or autism,[3,4] most of the known CNVs do not seem to be associated with any single neurodevelopmental disorder. Even within a single family, the same genetic lesion appears to be associated with different mental or developmental disorders. And even though these may be huge mutations, some CNVs by themselves have subtle effects unless there is a second insult such as a second mutation or an environmental influence.[5] As we look closer, it's clear that there are many different forms of variation in the genome and many potential genomic roads to mental disorder. So many, that some scientists have taken to quoting Tolstoy's opening to Anna Karenina: "All happy families are alike; each unhappy family is unhappy in its own way."

26. Scientists have recently isolated some genes associated with several mental disorders. According to Dr. Insel in this passage, which of the following is NOT one of these?
    E. Attention deficit hyperactivity disorder
    F. Obsessive-compulsive disorder
    G. Autism spectrum disorders
    J. Bipolar disorder

27. Recent research has connected copy number variations (CNVs) with serious mental illnesses. What is true about these CNVs?
    A. They are common genomic variations
    B. They involve only deleted segments
    C. They involve only genomic duplications
    D. They may tend to cause more disease

28. According to Dr. Insel, what has research thus far found regarding large genetic mutations known as copy number variations (CNVs)?
    F. Most identified CNVs are associated with specific mental disorders
    G. In the same family, the same genetic lesion creates the same illness
    H. CNVs can sometimes be found to be limited to within a single family
    J. They are no more prevalent in people with certain mental disorders

29. Which of the following is correct about copy number variations (CNVs), according to this excerpt?
    A. Because these genetic mutations are huge in size, their effects are always huge
    B. In spite of their enormous size, these mutations only ever cause subtler effects
    C. CNVs have milder effects if combined with other genetic/environmental factors
    D. Some CNVs have milder effects when there are not other contributing variables

30. Dr. Insel states that "...some scientists have taken to quoting Tolstoy's opening to Anna Karenina: "All happy families are alike; each unhappy family is unhappy in its own way." Which is the *best* explanation for how this relates to his discussion?
    E. Unhappy families represent those with mental disorders showing great individual variation.
    F. Tolstoy wrote Anna Karenina in 1870s Russia, where inbreeding caused much mental illness.
    G. Happy families represent those that have no mental disorders and are genetically identical.
    J. In general there is more natural variation among unhappy families than among happy ones.

Answers and Explanations

English Test

<u>Passage I</u>

1. B: The rest of the paragraph is written in the past tense. The other choices are all present tense.

2. G: The author wishes to emphasize that the area where the Wampanoag lived was not called Massachusetts at that time. The other choices do not do that.

3. A: This is an example of an introductory word coming before the main clause and set off by a comma, for emphasis. Answers B and D differ in meaning from the original text.

4. G: The expression joins an independent clause to a dependent one, so a comma is not required. Answers F and H are redundant, since "and" and "also" have similar meaning.

5. C: No verb follows "animals" which, like "forest" is an indirect object, so no comma is needed. Answer B is needlessly wordy.

6. F: This is the possessive pronoun. The sentence makes no sense with any of the other spellings.

7. C: This gives the sentence a parallel construction of elements that modify the noun "stories." Answer A is grammatically correct but reads with less clarity.

8. G: This is the most specific as well as the simplest. While the statement may be true for Indians in general, the article is about the Wampanoag.

9. B: The clause beginning in "but" is independent, so that a comma is required.

10. J: The original sentence includes two independent clauses, which must be separated by a comma and one of seven coordinating conjunctions: *and, but, for, or, nor, so, yet*. Alternatively, they may be split into two sentences, as is done for answer J. Answer G contains the redundancy "and...also."

11. C: The elements of a list require separation by commas.

12. J: This gives a construction parallel to "from land.".

13. B: This causes the verb "growing" to be compared to "hunting" rather than to the noun "animals." As written, the sentence implies that the animals were grown.

14. G: The phrase is completely unnecessary to understand the meaning of the sentence.

15. B

<u>Passage II</u>

16. H: This phrase tells the reader where the man appeared. Answer F creates a run-on sentence,

- 70 -

answer is Gredundant, and choice J creates a disagreement of verb tense.

17. B: The original and answer C are slang usage, and D, suggesting that the villagers had only then noticed the monkeys, is inappropriate.

18. G: As the clause following the conjunction *and* is dependent, the comma is not employed.

19. D: The action described in the portion of the sentence following the conjunction is contrary to expectation, since the villagers hunted less despite the generous payments, and *but* reflects that contradiction better than any of the other choices.

20. J: The correct spelling for the possessive pronoun.

21. C: This implies that the action that follows is a consequence of the one that precedes, i.e., the man raised his price because the villagers were losing interest.

22. F: No comma is used to set off a dependent clause.

23. C: This is an adjective indicating finite supply. Answer A is an adverb, inappropriate for modifying a noun.

24. G: This avoids splitting the infinitive "to see" while maintaining the emphasis provided by "even."

25. C: This proper use of the infinitive also maintains parallel structure with "to see," which appears earlier in the same sentence.

26. G: A semi-colon may be used to join two sentences when they are of similar content.

27. D: Using the subjective pronoun *he* with the verb *to be*. Answers B and C create a repetitive structure within the paragraph.

28. G: This uses the subjective pronoun *I* with the verb *to be*.

29. C: The past tense is needed since the story is set in the past. Answer D is slang usage.

30. F: The comma appropriately sets off the ending clause and adds emphasis. Answer G is a run-on sentence, while H and J introduce changes in meaning.

Passage III
31. B: The subject noun "staff" is a collective singular noun, taking the singular form of the auxiliary verb "was" rather than the plural "were."

32. H: The noun "outing" begins with a vowel and thus takes the indefinite article "an" rather than "a."

33. C: The correct form is "supposed to" rather than "suppose to"; "...was supposed to" is the past perfect tense of the reflexive "to be supposed," i.e., to be presumed or expected [to do something].

34. J: "To also go" is a split infinitive. Modifier placement: either "on the trip" or "with them" should follow "to go"; whichever is used first, the other should come next ("on the trip with them" or "with them on the trip"). The modifier "also," used as an adverb, goes either at the beginning ("Jacques also was supposed to go…" or "Jacques was also supposed to go…," not offered as choices) or at the end.

35. B: Dangling participle. The van was not driving up the street; Jacques was, so the subject and verb indicating this are needed.

36. H: "There" is the adverb modifying the verb "got" and indicating place. "Their" is the possessive form of the plural pronoun "they." "They're" is a contraction of "they are," a pronoun and a verb, and is always spelled with an apostrophe.

37. D: The verb phrase "had already gone" is the past perfect tense of the verb "to go." "Were…going" is the past progressive tense and "are…gone" is the present perfect. The former changes the meaning of the sentence and the latter does not agree in tense with the rest of the sentence ("…got there…found out…").

38. G: "Their" is the possessive form of the plural pronoun "they." "They're" is a contraction of the pronoun "they" and the verb "are." "They" does not have the possessive form needed to modify the noun "trip."

39. A: "Specialists'" is the correct possessive plural form of the noun. "Specialist's" is the possessive singular form. The form "specialists" is plural but not possessive. "Specialist" is singular and not possessive.

40. G: "Me" is the correct form of the pronoun when it is part of the modifying prepositional phrase "with…me" rather than "with…I." Other pronouns "we" and "them" change the meaning.

Mathematics Test

1. B: To solve, line up the like terms, as follows:

$$
\begin{array}{r}
3x^2 + x + 3 \\
+\quad 8x^2 + 5x + 16 \\
\hline
11x^2 + 6x + 19
\end{array}
$$

2. J: Out of the twelve numbers, half are even. That means there is a 50% chance that the spinner will land on an even number.

3. C: To find perimeter, add the sides.

4. H: A straight line is 180°. Subtract to solve: 180° - 45° = 135°

5. A: Lines 1 and 2 are parallel. If the parallel lines continued on into infinity, they would never cross. To *intersect* means that the lines cross. *Bisect* means that a line cuts another line or figure in two equal halves. To *correspond* means to match.

6. K: The degree measurement for alternate interior angles is exactly the same. In the figure, there

- 72 -

are two pairs of alternate interior angles: B and C; A and D.

7. D: An obtuse angle is one that is more than 90° (a right angle) and less than 180°. Answer choices A, B and C are not angles. Answer choice E, angle B, is an acute angle since it is small than a 90° angle.

8. G: 410 ml x 4 containers = 1640 ml
Change to liters: 1640 ÷ 1000 = 1.64
Add the liter that was already in the pot: 1.64 + 1 = 2.64 liters

9. E: To solve:
8 x 1 = 8
8 x 2 = 16
8 x 3 = 24
8 x 4 = 32
8 x 5 = 40

10. K: There should be one number in the ones place, then all other numbers after the decimal. Count the numbers that have been moved past the decimal. That is the number that is placed in a superscript beside the number 10. If you then multiplied, you would be left with the original number.

11. A: Simplify the fraction by dividing both the numerator and the denominator by their greatest common factor. In this case, the greatest common factor is 11. When you do that, 44/99 becomes 4/9.

12. J: Snappy Twisters are the only ones that fall into the criteria listed in the question. The use of the words "no more than" is important to notice.

13. D: In math, a ray is a straight line extending out from a point. Answer choice C shows a straight line.

14. J: If all of the children are girls, and some of the girls like soccer, then some of the children must like soccer. None of the other statements can be deduced from the information given.

15. D: Find the common denominator for the two fractions so that you can compare them. You can use the common denominator of 45, as follows:
2/5 = 18/45
4/9 = 20/45
Look at the numerators: 18 and 20. The number halfway between them is 19, so the answer is 19/45

16. J: You would need 7 cases because 15 x 7 = 105. You would have some extra room in the last case, but 6 cases would only give you room for 90 and you need to be able to fit 100 ring boxes into cases.

17. A: The fraction of ½ is the same as 50%. None of the other fractions are equal to that.

18. F: 250 ÷ 5 = 50

- 73 -

All of the other divisors leave a remainder, as follows:
$250 \div 15 = 16$ r. 10
$250 \div 20 = 12$ r. 10
$250 \div 30 = 8$ r. 10
$250 \div 75 = 3$ r. 25

19. B: The average of 7 and x is 7 + x divided by 2. The average of 9, 4, and x is 9 + 4 + x divided by 3. (7+x)/2 = (9+4+x)/3. Simplify the problem and eliminate the denominators by multiplying the first side by 3 and the second side by 2. For the first equation, (21 + 3x)/6. For the second equation, (18 + 8 + 2x)/6. Since the denominators are the same, they can be eliminated, leaving 21 + 3x = 26 + 2x. Solving for x gets x = 26-21. x = 5.

20. J: This is a simple average problem. If x denotes Annie's score, 86+98+90+x, divided by 4 equals 92. To solve, multiply each side by 4 and add the known scores together to get 274 + x = 368. Subtract 274 from 368 to solve for x. x = 94.

21. D: If 3x - 2 = 1, then 3x = 3. Therefore, x = 1.

22. F: 2^4 = 2 x 2 x 2 x 2 = 16. Therefore, 4^x = 16; x = 2.

23. D: Solving for y in the second equation gives y = 4x-5. If we plug this into the first equation we get 2x + 3(4x-5) = 13. Solving for this equation gives us 14x = 28, or x = 2. Then, plug the value of x into either equation to solve for y. y = 3. Therefore, 3x + 2y = 12.

24. J: To solve this we express 30/100 x 2x in the lowest terms: 3x/5.

25. E: There are 7 integers whose absolute value is less than 4: -3, -2, -1, 0, 1, 2, 3.

26. J: The sum of two negative numbers is a negative number.

27. B: The perimeter of a square is four times the length of any one of its sides. If a square's perimeter is 20, the length of any side is 5. The perimeter of this rectangle is six times the length of a side, which is 30.

28. H: The percentage of freshmen studying history, engineering, or Spanish is 30 + 25 + 17 = 72. Therefore, the percentage of freshmen studying something else is 100 – 72. The percentage is 28%.

29. D: Since class size is the same for all four years, we can average to get the percentage of the overall student body studying history. (30 + 33 + 36 + 29)/4 = 32%.

30. J: The percentage of juniors majoring in Spanish is 14. The percentage of juniors majoring in history is 36. 14/36 in lowest terms is 7/18.

Reading Test

Prose Fiction

1. C: He feels comfortable that he has fooled the police by hiding the evidence of his crime. The police are investigating a neighbor's report of the victim's scream, not just visiting. He feels proud of

covering up his deed, but he also feels guilt, which (along with his madness) explains his growing paranoia. He is in denial of his guilty feelings, so they are indirectly manifested through the sound he hears and what he thinks it is.

2. J: The narrator feels he has hidden his act from the police, but is so haunted by his guilt that he is bound to give himself away eventually. Fear of being discovered is his primary motivation in wishing the police gone, not merely an overlong stay, irritation at their conversation, fatigue from his earlier labors to hide the victim's body, or an unjustified police visit. The latter is justified, and the former three are all secondary to his overriding guilt and fear.

3. B: The headache and ringing in the ears the narrator suffers are caused by his extreme psychological distress, not by a medical condition, the conversation, extended questioning, or a cold. He begins by acting chatty and "normal" with the police, but "ere long," he finds he cannot tolerate keeping up the pretense. The ringing in his ears then develops into the sound that torments him.

4. J: The narrator's heart was beating ever harder as the strain of hiding the truth of his guilt increased. Because he was in denial of his guilt, he projected the sound of his heart beating onto the victim's heart, even though the victim was dead. (Note: denial and projection are Freudian concepts. Poe predated and anticipated Freud.) The sound was not in the room, outside of the building, or under the floorboards as the victim was dead. It was also not entirely imaginary; rather, in his dissociated state (another Freudian concept), he did not recognize it as his own heartbeat.

5. A: The narrator did murder the victim. This can be deduced from the excerpted information, especially his confession at the end. (It is also directly stated earlier in the story, outside of the excerpted passage.) The killer was not another; the narrator is not imagining the corpse; at this point in the story, the officers are not yet aware of the corpse; and the narrator is not mistaken about where the corpse is located.

6. G: The narrator's actions were attempts to distract the police from the sound he thought would incriminate him. He was not actually infuriated; Poe's use of "*as if* excited to fury" indicates this. He was not trying to distract the men from their own observations, but from the sound he heard and found incriminating. The police were not obviously suspicious. The narrator is paranoid, but he does not conclude that the police suspect or know anything until later in this paragraph. At the point quoted in the question, he was not very calm but was feeling increasing anxiety.

7. D: The narrator was desperately trying to keep the police from hearing what he heard. The character Poe created was indeed clearly insane, but this was not the only reason for his actions, and not the immediate reason. It was not the police's questions as much as his own internal state that caused his agitation. Though he wished they would leave, his foaming, raving, and swearing were deliberate attempts, primarily to divert their attention from the sound he believed would give him away, not primarily to make them leave. The narrative does not describe his using these same behaviors throughout the passage.

8. H: Until his confession, the police did not suspect or know what the narrator had done, and they were not mocking him. These were all figments of his imagination. They were not pretending not to know. They were not suspicious and were not trying to entrap him. Out of his inner guilt, the narrator leapt to these conclusions. "...this I thought, and this I think" shows that his insanity was not temporary, but permanent. Even as he begins the story insisting he is "not mad," he

demonstrates his madness throughout the narrative.

9. A: Poe effectively uses repetition to drive his points home. Note the repetition in the second paragraph of the words "sat," "still," and "chatted"; "continued" and "became more distinct"; the clauses "this I thought, and this I think"; the consecutive sentences, "But **anything was** better **than this** agony! Anything was** more tolerable **than this** derision!"; his seven repetitions near the end of "Louder!"; "here, here"; etc. Elaboration, great detail, and wordiness are opposites of Poe's literary techniques in this story: he is very economical with words, avoiding superfluous details and descriptions to focus on the main character's obsession and paranoia. In this excerpt (as in the entire short story), there is no dialogue at all except for the narrator's single-sentence exclamation at the very end.

10. G: The narrator had mistaken the sound of his own heart, beating wildly from the stress of his "horror," anxiety, and guilt, for the victim's heart, which he irrationally imagined was still beating. The victim was not buried alive and his heart was not still beating. The murderer was not hearing memories of the victim's heartbeat. While he was delusional, the narrator did not create the sound where there was nothing; rather, he imagined his heartbeat was the victim's heartbeat. The police did not simulate the sound. They knew nothing of the murder until the murderer gave himself away. Poe uses the narrator's projection of his heartbeat onto the victim's heart to illustrate how he is trapped by his own guilt as his psyche externalizes his internal state.

Social Science

11. A: As Freud points out, some wish-fulfillment dreams can be dreams "of convenience" addressing a need without the dreamer having to awaken and act to meet them. However, he also notes that in some cases, a wish-fulfillment dream will not satisfy a physical need like thirst. He never writes anything about dreams making wishes come true that actions cannot. He does remark in the first sentence of this excerpt that some wish-fulfillment dreams are easy to understand.

12. G: In the description following the phrase quoted in the question, the author describes how he is able to make himself have the dream again by inducing thirst. To evoke the dream does not mean to wipe it from his memory, to describe it while awake, to remember it in its entirety, or to change it next time he has it.

13. C: Freud mentions that his "thirst for revenge upon Otto and Dr. M" can be satisfied by a dream as he comments that unlike this thirst for revenge, his thirst for water cannot also be satisfied by dreaming of drinking water. He only mentions eating salty food when he is awake, as it makes him thirsty later, awakening him. He does not find a need to wake up satisfied by dreaming about it. He dreams of the urn partly because it is gone, but does not say the dream satisfies his need to get it back.

14. J: A cinerary urn is an urn used to hold the ashes of a deceased person who has been cremated. It is not used to empty fireplaces or collect oven cinders. Although a salty taste could be a dream manifestation of physical thirst according to this excerpt, in this case Freud attributes it not *only* to thirst, but also specifically to ashes. He does not state that ashes tasting salty was an imaginary part of his dream.

15. D: He remarks that he [normally] sleeps well and is "not accustomed to being waked by a bodily need." He follows this thought logically to show that wish-fulfillment dreams can be convenient by

- 76 -

taking the place of action. However, he also notes this is not the case specifically with physical thirst. He does not state he is awakened frequently by thirst; that dreaming of drinking eliminates the need to awaken; or that thirst only wakes him when he is not dreaming—in fact, he states that his waking from thirst "is preceded by a dream." The dream is caused by real thirst, not vice versa.

16. J: Freud writes that he brought the urn home from Italy but subsequently gave it away. It was not only a dream object. He did not lose it or break it. It was not present but out of reach; this applies to his wife's water glass, which he could not reach without awakening and getting out of bed.

17. C: Because he had emptied his own water glass before going to sleep and could not reach his wife's glass without awaking and getting up, Freud explains that he dreamed "quite appropriately" that his wife was giving him a drink. His rationale for his dream's including the vase was because (a) it was "inaccessible" like his glass; and (b) having contained ashes of human remains, it would logically add salt to the water, and he associated a salty taste with his thirst. The urn had not belonged to his wife; Freud, not his wife, had brought it back from Italy; it was not on his wife's bed-table; and she was not using it as a water glass.

18. G: In this context, Freud refers to the ego as the sense of self. He confirms his meaning of egoistic as self-serving in the sentence following "egoistic": "Love of comfort is really not compatible with consideration for others." While he described the ego as the reality principle in that it recognizes the reality of a situation, in this context egoistic does not mean truthful or realistic. Heroism is unrelated to this meaning. While people often use Freud's term "ego" to describe conceited people, he does not use it that way here. (Freud might have described conceit as an "inflated ego.")

19. A: Dream symbols by nature are not literally the same as what they represent. The wife's water glass was only "inaccessible" while Freud lay in bed, which his dream reflected. The dream symbolized the glass with the urn, which was even more physically inaccessible as he had given it away and no longer had it. Both objects were not in the bedroom but out of reach; only the glass was. The urn was not in the room and the glass was; hence only the urn was no longer present. Both objects were real and not just figments of his dream.

20. J: Freud does make the point that dreams as wish-fulfillment actually serve a purpose and perform a function. He does not find they always eliminate the need for action. For example, he states that a dream can satisfy his need for revenge, so it is not ineffective in that case. But he also notes that "Unfortunately," dreaming of drinking water does not satisfy thirst; so in that case, it does not eliminate the need to act. In the case of thirst, he finds a wish-fulfillment dream alerts him to a need by waking him; but in the case of revenge, he finds that a wish-fulfillment dream can indeed meet the need without waking him.

Humanities

21. C: Browne's orthography reflects the state of the English language in the seventeenth century. English was in a period of transition from Elizabethan English to Modern English. The variant spellings and inconsistencies are not the results of having no editor, of individual idiosyncratic forms, or any affectations on the part of the author; Browne was born and lived in England, and English was his first language.

22. G: In ancient times, the prevailing belief was that the sun revolved around the earth, meaning a

- 77 -

belief in a geocentric universe. Copernicus challenged this, proposing that the earth moves and revolves around the sun, and was later proven correct. At the time Browne was writing *Religio Medici,* Copernicus' hypotheses were not widely accepted and were still publicly controversial. He was not simply correcting Copernicus' prepositional usage. He was not comparing Copernicus' opinion of happiness with his own. Copernicus did not theorize that the sun moved, so Browne was not referring to a nonexistent theory. Browne's reference does not concern religious beliefs about the location of heaven or happiness.

23. D: Browne's reference is to the Old Testament book of Ecclesiastes, wherein the statement, "Vanity of vanities, saith the Preacher, vanity of vanities; all is vanity" (Ecclesiastes 1.2), is attributed to King Solomon, son of King David. This quotation was not from the *Song of Solomon,* also known as the *Song of Songs* or *Canticles.* Browne was not using his own words to describe Solomon's ideas as he specifically wrote "All is vanitie," which is verbatim one of the most frequent translations. He was not quoting a Biblical scholar and was not quoting a sermon.

24. F: He meant that felicity or happiness is not found in things that humankind, or the world, adores. He did not mean that being loved by the world does not bring happiness. He did not mean that people in the world who are loved do not attain grace. He did not mean that finding favor from the world does not guarantee happiness. He did not mean that things loved by the planet are lacking in virtue. He meant that happiness is not found in things of this world, or "that [which] the world adores."

25. D: *Summum bonum* is Latin for "the highest good." Aristotle was Greek, but he lived close to 2,000 years before Browne. Aristotle's works were translated by later scholars into Latin, as was the Bible. The phrase *summum bonum,* first seen in 1563, was used by St. Thomas Aquinas and others in theological and philosophical writings. As a medical doctor and a Biblical, religious, scientific, and literary scholar, Browne knew Latin and was familiar with Aristotle's work.

26. H: He means Aristotle's idea of the *summum bonum* is not believable, even impossible, and is a fantasy. The literal meaning of Chimera is a monster from Greek mythology, a female figure having a lioness' head and body, a tail with a snake's head on its end, and a goat's head growing out of its back. However, this word has also developed the figurative meaning of an idea or fantasy that is foolish and difficult or impossible to believe. This meaning is common in the English literary lexicon, and this is how Browne used it here.

27. D: Any agents of people's happiness are not included by Browne in his definition. He finds happiness to be synonymous with anything in which "God himself" and "the holy Angels" are happy and "the Devils" are unhappy; and whatever is conducive to these ("whatsoever conduceth unto this") is also synonymous with or can be called happiness ("may with an easie Metaphor deserve that name").

28. J: Browne does not wish to be loved for his desires and ambitions. He uses the words "desires" and "ambition" in the sentence following the sentence describing what he asks as blessings, but not in that context or with that meaning. He does ask to be blessed with a clear conscience, control over his feelings, the love of God ("thyselfe"), and the love of his best friends.

29. B: By this expression, Browne means he will be so extremely happy (if God blesses him with the things he asks) that he will be able to feel sorry for the most famous Emperor of the Roman Empire, who enjoyed perhaps the greatest power, wealth, fame, and prestige in the known Western world at

the time. He does not mean total happiness is prerequisite to pitying others; that Caesar was not happy; that he will be happier than Caesar; or that pitying Caesar will make him happier.

30. F: By contrasting "done" and "undoing," Browne places literary emphasis on the idea that God's will supersedes man's will, so that fulfilling the former could undo the latter and it would still be right. He did not mean that his own life had been ruined, or that his undoing was required, either by God or by himself, for God's will to be done. He did not mean that his life opposed God's will. Implicit in the sentence is the idea that God's will be done *even though* it *might* be his own undoing.

ScienceTest

PART A

1. C: The ants were most likely confused by a chemical barrier. The first text paragraph states that ants communicate "even if they can't see one another," and that they do this by "sending chemical messages to one another." A visual barrier is less likely as the text emphasizes that ants do not rely on seeing one another. The student who performs this experiment will find the ants can go around or over a physical barrier like a pebble; and an auditory barrier like noise will not stop them. They would not be "confused by a coordination barrier'; rather, their coordination would be confused by a chemical barrier like window cleaner, which removes their chemical messages.

2. G: The passage states that Theodor Engelmann conducted the experiment it then describes in 1883. Therefore he conducted it in the nineteenth century, not the twentieth century, which would be in the 1900s; not the eighteenth century, which would be in the 1700s; not the seventeenth century, which would be in the 1600s; and not the sixteenth century, which would be in the 1500s.

3. D: It is not true that single-celled organisms can only respond individually and separately. The passage indicates that single-celled organisms not only can respond to environmental stimuli such as light, gravity, or chemicals, but also can organize their responses and work together to benefit them all.

4. J: In this context, Spirogyra is a genus of green alga (plural = algae), a filamentous, freshwater organism with a simple cellular structure and hundreds of species. In another context, there is a British (folk-rock) musical group named Spirogyra and an American (jazz fusion) musical group named Spyro Gyra. The bacterial cells in the experiment described in this passage were E. coli, which consume oxygen from sources like algae. The spectrum is the rainbow of colors created by different wavelengths of light. White light with all the wavelengths can be broken down into its component colors by use of a prism, which refracts (bends) light.

5. A: Photosynthesis is the process of using energy from sunlight to produce the organism's own food, emitting oxygen as a waste product; bacteria like E. coli require oxygen to survive. Algae, plants, and some species of bacteria engage in photosynthesis. Those bacteria that do this do not use oxygen from algae to produce food. They use energy from sunlight to convert carbon dioxide to organic compounds like sugars for nourishment. Both types of organisms do not need both sun and oxygen to survive. Algae and some photosynthetic bacteria need sunlight for photosynthesis; the E. coli bacteria described need oxygen to survive. Bacteria do not produce oxygen, creating food for algae; algae produce oxygen, creating food for bacteria. Algae do not take in oxygen and expel carbon dioxide as humans do in breathing; algae take in carbon dioxide and expel oxygen.

6. H: The back part of the human brain, or the hindbrain, is most similar to the brains of simpler animals. It contains the cerebellum, which regulates voluntary motor movements, balance and equilibrium, and muscle tone; and the amygdala, a part of the limbic system, involved in processing emotions. The front part of the human brain, or forebrain, is the most dissimilar to the brains of simpler animals. It contains the cerebrum. The middle part or midbrain regulates eye movements and physical reflexes. All parts of the human brain are not equally most similar to simpler animal brains. It is not true that none of these parts is most similar to simpler animal brains.

7. A: The hippocampus is the structure that helps to transfer short-term memories to long-term memories, the kind that last and can be retrieved later. The hypothalamus is a brain structure with multiple functions, including sending information to the pituitary gland, regulating emotions, and stimulating waking from sleep and the flow of adrenaline. Its location is identified in the top diagram here. The amygdala is active in emotional reactions, the secretion of hormones, and the storage of memories related to emotional responses. The cerebellum, identified in the top diagram at the back of the brain, regulates voluntary motor movements, balance and equilibrium, and muscle tone. The corpus callosum, also identified in the top diagram, is the structure that connects the left and right hemispheres of the brain so they can communicate and interact.

8. J: The cerebrum is the largest part of the brain, comprising 85 percent of its volume. Its convolutions, or folds and wrinkles, increase its surface area even more. It is responsible for higher cognitive functions. The corpus callosum is a long central body of tissue running between the left and right hemispheres of the brain and connecting them. The cerebellum is located at the rear of the brain and is responsible for motor control. The brainstem is the hindmost, lowest part of the brain that connects to the spinal cord. It contains the pons and the medulla oblongata. It controls functions necessary to survival like breathing, heart rate, blood pressure, digestion, and alertness. The amygdala plays important roles in emotions and memories, but is almond-shaped and of small size.

9. D: The imaging of thinking about words shows three regions with activity far apart from one another, and the amounts of activity (i.e., the sizes of the red parts) are larger than in the other images. The image for speaking words shows a smaller red area surrounded by yellow (yellow indicates lighter activity than red) with three separate yellow areas much smaller than those in the thinking about words image. The image for hearing words shows activity in one large area of connected parts. The image for seeing words shows a small active area in the occipital lobe (at the rear), which processes visual signals, with the rest and majority of activity farther forward. These images do not include one for "learning" words.

10. G: The image for speaking words shows all of the activity in one portion of the brain, which incorporates more than one structure and region, but these are all connected. The images for hearing, seeing, and thinking about words all show separate areas with activity. It is not true that none of the active areas looks contiguous; the one for speaking words does.

11. D: This excerpt indicates that geologic mapping is used to locate natural resources, such as mineral deposits, and to project the expenses associated with getting them out of the ground. It is also used to predict earthquakes, volcanoes, and other natural disasters; to evaluate the quality of ground water and detect contamination; to identify landfills and other buried waste sites; and to aid with land management and* planning efforts.

12. H: The Geological Information System (GIS) has seen changes in recent decades via the introduction of new software programs that allow mappers electronically to save and work with data on geologic features and relate these data to the full range of other types of data. This change has been more significant than any changes in the earth's surface or bedrock, which typically take far longer than decades. This excerpt mentions the costs of digging and slopes lacking stability, but in terms of identifying them rather than in terms of changes in them.

13. B: Basalt is not present in the graphic shown. This sample geologic map identifies shale, granite, limestone, and sandstone as existing in the mapped area. Shale, limestone, and sandstone are sedimentary rocks formed from layered mineral deposits, while basalt and granite are igneous rocks formed from cooled volcanic magma. Granite is rich in quartz and forms when magma cools slowly, while basalt is rich in magnesium and iron and forms when magma cools more quickly.

14. J: The only areas on the map labeled with the symbol for radon gas are the two areas of shale, a type of sedimentary rock, and the area of granite, an igneous rock. Radon is a naturally occurring noble gas that is radioactive and can kill those exposed to it. The areas with petroleum-bearing sandstone, water-bearing sandstone, sand and gravel, and limestone are not identified as having radon gas.

15. A: The rock types found in different areas are represented on the map by different colors, not by symbols. Areas where landslides occur; fault lines (cracks in the earth) that produce earthquakes; areas of land subsidence (downward shifting of land toward sea level, secondary to faults as on this map, or to mining, ground water, natural gas removal, dissolving limestone, etc.); and areas containing radioactive elements (radon gas in this case) are all represented by symbols, which are identified in the legend or key below the map.

PART D
16. H: The Earth's Moon is a natural satellite, as described in the excerpt. A satellite is a body, natural or man-made, that revolves around a larger body in space. It is not a meteoroid, which is a fragment of matter that vaporizes when too close to a space body having an atmosphere. It is not an asteroid, which is a rocky space object that can from be a few hundred feet to several hundred miles wide. In Earth's solar system, the majority of asteroids are in a belt between Mars and Jupiter. The Earth's Moon is not a comet, which is a frozen mass of dust and gas with a defined orbit. It is not a planet, which is a space body orbiting a star and has enough mass for its gravity to round its shape, but not enough mass to cause thermonuclear fusion as occurs in the sun and other stars.

17. A: The shape of our solar system is elliptical, i.e., an elongated, closed curve. It is not rectangular as it has no right angles. It is not spherical or round. It is not spiral-shaped like some galaxies such as the Spiral Nebula. (Our solar system is in the Milky Way galaxy.) It is not triangular; its shape is made of curved arcs rather than straight lines.

18. J: The passage states that the Sun makes up 99.8% of the total mass of our solar system, which is nearly all of it. Our Sun's mass is a far greater proportion of the solar system's total mass than half (50%), two thirds (67%), four fifths (80%), or three quarters (75%) of it.

19. D: Our Sun exerts its gravity on all planets, satellites (like moons), asteroids, meteoroids, and comets in its vicinity, pulling them into orbit around the Sun. The Sun's mass is so much greater than any other body in our solar system that it attracts all five of these types of objects, not just one, two, three, or four of them.

20. G: The passage does not mention anything about the planets in our solar system being formed out of the remains of meteor showers. Some astronomers believe that all of the planets in our solar system formed out of one large flat gas cloud. Others believe that some very large celestial body, in passing close to the Sun, pulled a stream of gas off of the Sun's surface, and that the planets formed out of the separated stream of gases.

PART E

21. C: What Newton named centripetal force is an opposing force to the tendency of moving objects to follow straight-line paths. Without gravity, the planets would move in straight lines; gravity pulls them into curved paths. Centripetal force causes objects to move toward their orbital centers, not to recede away from them. Newton notes the similarity of magnetism in metals and gravitational pull in the Earth as both involve central attraction; they are not opposites. A stone swung around in a sling tends to recede from the hand swinging it, while centripetal force attracts the stone toward the hand, not vice versa.

22. F: Newton defines centripetal force as one that opposes the natural tendency of orbiting bodies to move away from the center. It does not complement or complete this tendency; it does not augment or increase it; it does not support it; and it is not a collateral force, i.e., related to, but less important than, this natural tendency.

23. B: Newton describes the motion of a projectile in the absence of gravitational force as flying out in a straight line, not straight up into the air or straight down to the ground. He notes that if the resistance of the air were eliminated, it would follow a uniform motion and a straight line. Therefore without gravity or air's resistance, it would not show variations in motion. Newton describes the natural motion of projectiles in the absence of gravity and air resistance as a constant, so the means of projection would not affect it. (The angle of projection would set the trajectory of the straight line.)

24. J: Newton explains that the distance the lead ball projectile travels will increase in equal proportion to the increase in velocity, but only if the resistance of the atmosphere is also eliminated. Otherwise, air resistance would keep the increase in distance from matching the increase in speed. With air resistance eliminated, doubling velocity will not increase the projectile's distance tenfold; increase in distance traveled will match increase in speed.

25. D: Newton speculates that given sufficient velocity, a projected object like a lead ball shot with gunpowder could travel all the way around the Earth before falling. He also writes in this passage that the line it followed would become less curved, not more; and that it could fall at various angles, not a constant one, depending on how far it went and how much the curve was diminished. Therefore it would not always behave the same. Newton further proposes herein that with force creating sufficient velocity, the lead ball he describes could even fly far enough to leave Earth's atmosphere and reach outer space, where its motion could continue indefinitely with no gravity or atmosphere to stop it.

PART F

26. G: Insel does not name obsessive-compulsive disorder as one of the mental disorders for which genes have been identified. He does state that researchers have found genes associated with attention deficit hyperactivity disorder, autism spectrum disorders, bipolar disorder, and schizophrenia.

27. D: Dr. Insel reports here that some CNVs, which can involve millions of different DNA bases, are thought to be more penetrant, i.e., more likely to cause disease, than single-base mutations that do not greatly increase disease risk. CNVs are not common but are also not small in numbers: while thousands of different CNVs have been identified, each one is rare, and Insel emphasizes this by italicizing the word "rare." CNVs do not involve only deleted segments of genomes, or only duplicated segments; they can involve either deletions or duplications of genomic segments.

28. H: Insel reports that researchers have found some CNVs to exist only within one family. However, what puzzles scientists is that the same genetic lesion in members of the same family seems to cause various developmental or mental disorders rather than the same illness. It is not true that CNVs are no more prevalent in people with certain mental disorders: Insel states that they are ten times as likely to be found in people with schizophrenia or autism. The known CNVs are not all found in more than one individual: as Insel writes, some CNVs develop "de novo" (anew) in just a single person.

29. D: According to this excerpt, some CNVs have only "subtle" effects on individuals if no other variables are added, such as another genetic mutation or some environmental influence. Thus, though CNVs are generally huge mutations, their effects are not always accordingly huge. However, it is not correct that they only ever cause subtler effects; some do, and some can cause more significant problems as they are suspected of being more penetrant (likely to cause illness). CNVs do not necessarily have milder effects if combined with other genetic or environmental factors; some of those factors magnify the effects of CNVs, as Dr. Insel has described. He also remarks that some scientists believe CNVs to be responsible for more variation than single-base mutations, even though more than 38,000 CNVs have been identified while many more—millions—of single-base mutations have been researched.

30. F: In this context, Insel means that scientists use this quotation referring to familial mental disorders to show the great variation found both in genomes and in genomic influences on mental illness. Historically, inbreeding did contribute to mental disorders in Russia, but this was mainly among the royalty; moreover, though Insel does discuss genetic mutations in families, this answer choice does not explain the quotation's relationship to his discussion. While happy families can represent those without mental disorders in this context, such families are never genetically identical. (Only monozygotic twins, i.e., from the same egg, are genetically identical.) It cannot be said that there is generally more variation among unhappy than among happy families, as there is no proof for such a generalization; moreover, in this context, "happy" and "unhappy" families represent those without and with mental disorders. Insel's reference does not mean mental illness cannot be analyzed within families due to individual variation, which is not true.

GUARANTEED TO IMPROVE YOUR TEST SCORE

"Effective, Affordable, Guaranteed"

We offer study materials for over 1000 different standardized exams, including:

Business and Career Exams
Construction and Industry Exams
Counseling and Social Work Exams
Finance, Insurance, and Real Estate Exams

Medical and Nursing Exams
Teacher Certification Exams
K-12 Exams
College Prep Exams

At Mometrix, we take your study time very seriously. We realize how busy you are and want to give you the most effective tools possible so you can maximize the limited time you have to prepare. Our team of testing experts has devoted hours and hours scrutinizing every possible topic that could be covered on the exam to give you practice questions that are as much like the actual test as possible. Our thorough answer key not only shows you the right answers, but offers in-depth explanations to ensure that no matter how confusing the test questions are worded, you will understand the concepts well enough to choose the right answers. Understanding these practice questions will put you well on your way to the content mastery necessary to perform well on your exam. But you don't have to take our word for it; here is what some of our customers have to say:

"I just had to thank you guys for the test prep! I bought the guide as a last minute prep, I mean maybe 5 hours before the test. Like I said, I had ZERO preparation! I was nervous about the test, let alone receiving the score I needed. I read the guide through only once before test time and needless to say, the only way I passed was thanks to your refresher!!" - Brian

"I have just retaken my test and I scored way better than my previous score. I had this program for only 3 days and I just want to say that I can't believe how well it worked." - Mandy C.

"Just wanted to say thank you. Due to your product I was able to ace my exam with very little effort. Your tricks did the trick. Thanks again, and I would recommend this product to anyone." - Erich L.

"I just wanted to tell you I had ordered your Study Guide, and I finally aced the test after taking it numerous times. I tried tutors and all sorts of study guides and nothing helped. Your guide did the job and got me the score I needed! Thank you!" - Nicholas R.

ISBN 978-1-62120-046-8

For questions about bulk discounts or ordering through your company/institution, please contact our Institutional Sales Department at 888-248-1219 or sales@mometrix.com.

Visit www.MometrixCatalog.com for our full list of products and services.

Made in USA